a new
adventure
every
day

a new adventure every day

541 simple ways to live with pizzazz

David Silberkleit

SOURCEBOOKS, INC.
NAPERVILLE, ILLINOIS

Published by Sourcebooks, Inc.
P.O. Box 4410, Naperville, Illinois 60567-4410
(630) 961-3900
FAX: (630) 961-2168
www.sourcebooks.com

Library of Congress Cataloging-in-Publication Data

Silberkleit, David.
A new adventure every day: 541 simple ways to live with pizzazz / David Silberkleit.
     p. cm.
  ISBN 1-57071-946-2 (pbk.)
  1. Self-actualization (Psychology) I. Title.
  BF637.S4 S546 2002
  646.7—dc21

2002009636

Printed and bound in the United States of America
VHG   10   9   8   7   6   5   4   3   2   1

FOR RUBY

TABLE OF CONTENTS

"Security is mostly a superstition. It does not exist in nature, nor do the children of humankind as a whole experience it. Avoiding danger is no safer than outright exposure. Life is either a daring adventure or it is nothing at all."

—Helen Keller

introduction:
adventure
redefined

Traditionally, adventure has been defined as something primarily done by thrillseekers. Only people with the courage to risk life and limb have been worthy of an adventurous label. This is a book for everyone else. These pages are meant to support everyone who will never climb Everest, will probably never get behind the controls of an airplane, and perhaps will never even leave their time zone. This is a book for people who want to find adventure in everyday life.

In one of my recent adventurous-life workshops, a woman raised her hand before we started and sheepishly said, "I just want to make sure I'm in the right place, I mean, I'm not very adventurous, I'm not willing to jump out of an airplane or anything…" By the end of the evening, she was ready to start her own herb garden and to sign up for an adult-education painting class with one of her friends with whom she felt her relationship was stagnant. She had found ways to put her own unique adventurous life in place. Not the stuff of a Jacques Cousteau television special, but for her, it was living on the edge.

And that's what I hope to provide for you. After you read this book, your life won't look the same. You'll see your life with new eyes and discover numerous possibilities to create fun and excitement in places you would not have imagined. You'll start to see that your existing lifestyle is the perfect canvas for your adventurous spirit. You won't need any training, equipment, money, or plane tickets to create your everyday adventures. All you'll need is a new attitude and a willingness to see adventure as your undeniable right.

It took me half my life to realize that "adventurous" meant so much more than the stamps in my passport and the equipment in my closet. Adventure now means discovery of a unique new color of silver reflected in a cloud after sunset or a conversation with the person sitting next to me on a New York subway, just to see if maybe we have something in common. Adventure means asking my father what he remembers about being my age or telling my best friend something that I would never have dared to tell anyone before. Adventure means making something out of wood and offering it for sale in a gallery, even though I have never sold any artwork before.

There are few traditional adventures that I haven't tried. I've been a ski instructor, commercial glider and airplane pilot, scuba diver, sailboat racer, rock climber, and motorcyclist. I've traveled by bicycle in about a dozen different countries. I'm not someone you'll read about in record books, but in my first forty years, I certainly built what most people would call an adventurous life.

To my surprise, all my adventures led me to a lesson I hadn't expected. I discovered that I didn't need to go anywhere or plan any trips in order to be adventurous. Adventure was all around me, and rather than looking past it to get to the airport so I could find adventure out there, I discovered that I could find adventure any time right where I was. I found out that it didn't make any difference if I was sitting atop the highest point in Belize or in traffic on the New England Thruway. I discovered that life is inherently adventurous. Location is irrelevant. No matter where I am, it's up to me to create my own adventurous life. That's why this book describes adventures in your home, relationships, body, career, finances, and in nature. Start with simple steps in these areas and you'll find your whole life becoming more adventurous.

The human desire for adventure is insatiable. So it makes no sense to relegate adventure to just those two precious vacation weeks each year. It's during the other fifty weeks that adventure is waiting to be expressed. Don't compartmentalize your life so that adventure is reserved only for special occasions.

Go out into the world and reach for the most extreme adventures you can handle. See new cultures and try new sports and learn to parachute, if that excites you. This book is not meant to downplay explorers who single-handedly sail around the globe or climbers who make first ascents. These are wonderful and exciting adventures. It's just that such a small minority of people gets to experience adventure in this way. It's not that one kind of adventure is better than the other, it's just that they are distinct. And you need to appreciate the differences. They are each adventurous; it's just that one is exclusive and one is inclusive. It's the inclusive everyday adventures that I have written about in this book.

I made my whole life about traditional adventures only to discover that after a while it was no longer satisfying. But everyday adventures are an unlimited challenge. Every time I walk out the door, even on a trip to the mailbox, there's something new to discover.

The purpose of this book is to make you into that new kind of adventurer. I've taken apart everyday life and demonstrated ways anyone can find adventure, regardless of their lifestyle. This is an adventure guide that allows you to become an adventurer right now. You don't need to outfit yourself with expensive gear, extricate yourself from your everyday life, or take more time off. You can start your adventures right now, from exactly where you are.

I remember the first time I ever made a cross-country trip in a single-engine airplane in instrument conditions. I'll never forget the elation I experienced, descending to land at five hundred feet, as I popped out of the bottom of the cloud layer and there straight in front of me was the runway, right where it was supposed to be.

I don't think that elated feeling is from cheating death, because if I really had been at risk I wouldn't have taken off. But it's more elation from being completely alive. I was so fully immersed in this adventure because I knew that the consequences of a mistake were severe. That's what's missing in a life without everyday adventures. We live as though there are no consequences for tolerating our mundane lives, when in actuality, we die if we don't explore what is possible. Parked in front of a TV, it's easy to resign ourselves to the idea that life is only exciting for the people on the TV and not for the people watching.

So it's time for you to learn to fly. Not literally, although you might want to give it a try. I'm talking about being a pilot in your own everyday life. It's up to you to tune into your adventurous spirit and bring it out into the light. You don't ever have to go anywhere near an airplane. But don't miss out on your rightful opportunity to relish the adventure of being alive. In your short time on this Earth, look for ways to find adventure all around you and you'll start to experience that same elation that I felt after I landed, only you won't need the pilot's licenses that I worked so hard to acquire.

We live as if only the select few are out there risking their lives flying instrument approaches on rainy days. But the truth is that we never know which is the day that we will fly our last approach. There is no such thing as security, so you might as well make it up as you go along.

This book is about breaking down the polarity in our definition of adventure. Your first trip to ask your boss for a raise is your personal first ascent. Perhaps your instrument approach will happen in your bedroom with your spouse, when you finally ask for what you always wanted even though you have no idea what you'll get. When you go to your first yoga class, right in your neighborhood, that's your adventurous trip for the day. Once you start to see your life as an adventure, you can enjoy the traditional adventurer's journey without leaving town. You don't have to long for adventure and see yourself as somehow deficient for not being out there. Anyone can find challenge in his or her everyday experience.

THE PRINCIPLES OF EVERYDAY ADVENTURE

There are four basic principles woven into the pages of this book:

1. You are responsible for your own adventure; it's not up to a tour guide or anyone else to provide it. When you accept this fact, you break down the wall that normally separates mere mortals from the adventurers on the pages of adventure magazines.

2. There is more risk in living a sedentary life than a life full of fun and excitement. A life focused solely on safety consumes vitality. An adventurous life creates vitality. Adventure is a fuel that infuses us with energy and makes us feel more alive.

3. You are absolutely entitled to enjoy adventure in every day of your life no matter who or where you are. Even a housebound senior citizen can find new adventures by playing bridge with someone halfway around the globe on the Internet, learning to grow orchids at home, or cooking new ethnic cuisine.

4. Novelty is adventurous. Even the most mundane routine is an opportunity for adventure when you look for a new discovery along the way.

Even when a telemarketer interrupts your train of thought to sell you a newspaper you'll never read, you have a choice. You can scream and lose energy or engage the person on a relationship adventure and gain energy. Ask them their name. Speak to them in a funny accent. Ask them to tell you a story about the funniest thing that anyone ever said to them when they called. Ask them to tell you how it feels to be on the receiving end of so many slammed-down receivers.

When you speak to a telemarketer in this way, you are using the four principals to create an adventure: you're taking responsibility for creating adventure; you're choosing a fun path rather than playing it safe; you're grabbing adventure in an unexpected moment; and you're handling a routine annoyance in a brand-new way. This is how you make your everyday life adventurous. I hope this book will support you forever to search for opportunities to create these special adventures in the routine moments of your life.

In some cases, energy is not the benefit of adventure; discovery is. I didn't feel energized when my cat Ruby died while I was writing this book. But I felt that she had contributed to me in her death. I learned something about death from the experience. I resolved some questions about death from watching her die.

I experienced tremendous grief after the loss of my best friend of sixteen years. I hadn't realized the extent to which every movement in my life was so intertwined with that cat. As I fumbled for the light switch to enter my apartment, I did so with consciousness that Ruby was at my feet. When I woke up, my automatic response was to look to see where she had slept for the night. When I opened some yogurt in the morning, I automatically expected that she would rub against my leg when she heard that sound. After she died, I discovered how much I missed her each time I took such a routine action and noticed that my roommate was gone.

But I call this an adventure. I found a piece of myself I didn't know existed. I found new consciousness when I felt Ruby's spirit leave her body. And I found new capacity to look for her spirit in every piece of nature blossoming all around me. The experience motivated me to sign up for a hospice volunteer program, to learn even more about the adventure of death and to explore another piece of life that I had previously avoided. Ruby's death was not an energizing adventure as much as it was an inner adventure of self-discovery, one no less rich and exciting than any other adventure in this book.

But death is not the focus of this book; life is. And throughout these pages, you'll have a chance to inventory each domain of your life as you search for more adventure. There is nothing in this book that will require you to risk your life. Nowhere in this book do I suggest you should try parachuting, rock climbing, or scuba diving with sharks.

On the other hand, maybe you're already risking your life by working hard every day at something you hate, trying to build a secure financial future even though you live with chronic stress-related ailments. This pursuit of a secure successful lifestyle devoid of fun and excitement strikes me as the riskiest thing anyone can do.

HOW THIS BOOK GOT PUBLISHED

Something remarkable happened in the summer of 2000 that dramatically changed my relationship to adventure. I fell in love with a wonderful woman and launched a massive life change; perhaps one of my biggest adventures yet. I sold my home and most of its contents, and headed to Europe with just a tandem bicycle, saddlebags, and a small luggage trailer. Natalie and I planned to ride around Europe with no agenda other than to be together and discover the world. I brought a cell phone and laptop to keep in touch with coaching clients. The revenue from my coaching business would more than pay for our room and board at hostels and B&Bs. We set out from Dublin to begin a journey into the unknown.

After two months of beautiful cycling in Ireland, we boxed up our bike and headed to Holland, where we enjoyed warmer, drier, and flatter cycling for another month. And after that third month, it became clear that Natalie and I were not soulmates, as we had thought. Either that or three months on a tandem bike had killed our relationship. Regardless, we parted ways. I shipped the tandem bike home and bought a used single seater, hopped on a train with my saddlebags, and headed to France. I continued to coach clients as I toured France alone.

It was about a month into my solo travels that I had a startling revelation. I found myself asking people where was the best place to go in France and where I should head next to see the greatest scenery and biking that France had to offer. I suddenly realized that these four months of bicycling had all been spectacular. Whether we were in the so-called best counties of Ireland or the ones the guidebooks recommended bypassing, we had met incredible people and seen sights that we would not forget. It occurred to me that no matter where I went, there was an adventure to be had, and my ability to find adventure had nothing to do with my bike or my location; it had to do with my attitude. I had sold almost everything I owned and freed myself from all my commitments, other than to a handful of coaching clients, in order to have the time to enjoy my adventures out in the world. I realized that adventure was coming from inside of me and it made absolutely no difference where I was or what kind of vehicle I was riding. All of life is adventurous. And so I saw that there was no reason to stay out on the roads of Europe any longer. I decided it was time to head home and write about this discovery.

I stopped in Frankfurt to visit extended family and ultimately to fly back to New York. As it happened, the Frankfurt book fair coincided with my visit, so considering the divine circumstances that put the book fair in front of my nose on the end of one journey and the beginning of another, I headed to the massive convention center in clean clothes to look for a publisher.

I spent the morning being told that I was at the wrong show at the wrong time. This really wasn't the place for aspiring authors, especially those dressed in fleece and reflective yellow rain gear. I wandered around what must be the largest convention center in the world, looking for people who might like to publish what I had to say.

I was about ready to give up when, at a concession stand, I saw a woman eating a banana. "Where did you find fruit," I asked, "in a country that seems dedicated to putting bratwurst on every corner?"

She laughed, and even though she had brought the banana from home, she was interested in hearing why I was there. "Oh, you must meet Fred," she said, "he's in charge of the association of independent publishers." Moments later, Fred said that that I absolutely must speak with Dominique, the adventurous Sourcebooks publisher.

You are holding this book simply because I was adventurous enough to ask a woman at a concession stand, at a convention that might as well have been anywhere in the world, where she had gotten her banana.

adventure
on the
homefront

Y ou may tend to think that adventure only happens once you get on a plane and fly through a few different time zones. But your home can actually be the most adventurous part of your life. After all, you spend the most time there. So why not be your own in-house travel agent and design your apartment or your backyard to provide a wild adventure, whether you are walking up the stairs after dinner or simply parking your car in the garage? Your home and property can become your own paradise, without the pain of jet lag and the hassles of airport security.

Your home is likely a collection of conveniences coupled with a few things that you like. Turn that relationship on its ear. Take nothing for granted in your surroundings. Edit from your life that which does not inspire you and replace it with items and energies that feel adventurous. Engage the lifelong adventure of making all the ordinary objects in your home fun and exciting.

People often complain about their neighborhood and long for life in a more exciting community. I encourage clients to move all the time, but not before they have tried to optimize their own adventurous world right where they are. It's easy to blame your surroundings. It's quite another thing to take responsibility for getting what you need. You absolutely can create an adventurous world right in your backyard, no matter where you live.

I also find that people often decorate and provision their homes for an imaginary prospective buyer, who may one day come through the door with his realtor. Rather than live their own unique adventure, some people obsess about what the "marketplace" wants. That's one reason why many homes in America are not adventurous. People are afraid to take risks with what they perceive to be their biggest investment.

But your spirit should be your biggest investment. And even if the person who purchases your home has to bulldoze your golf driving range or repaint your garage floor, you'll get a much higher health and well-being dividend if you live in a house that fits you like your favorite denim shirt. Let your adventurous spirit run wild on your property. It's the one place in your life where you can always feel safe. And stop worrying about the next inhabitant of your house, who would have probably ripped up your conventional decor to make it more exciting anyway!

The adventures listed below are meant to bring forth the unique adventurous energy that lives inside of you. Transform your home into something completely new and unfamiliar. Go way outside of what is normal and into the unknown. Instead of traveling to the other side of the globe, go deep into your own living space on your own private customized adventure. Make your entire house into the ultimate piece of adventure gear that fits you and only you. And celebrate every free moment that you get to spend in your own special, adventurous world.

INDOORS

1 **Make the entrance** to your home the airlock in which you transition from the adventurous world outside into your fortified cave. Ring your entryway with storage bins and holders of your in-line skates and balaclavas. Display something Gore-Tex, even if you just wear it to walk your dog. Hang your backpack in plain view,

with caribeeners clipped to the outside, even if you have no idea what to do with them. Visit your local firehouse for inspiration. Leave your boots ready so that you can jump right into them and immediately save your newspaper from the cold. Or install your very own firefighter's pole.

2 **Give your keys** and cell phone their own miniature hangar in your entryway, ready for the next rescue flight in a storm. Or place them inside a Nepalese bowl or similar souvenir from Kathmandu, the starting point for an Everest ascent. Make your home feel like the headquarters of a mountain rescue team, but instead of ropes and ice axes in your foyer, make an adventurous display of the tools that support you throughout your adventurous day, even if it's just your keys, umbrella, and cell phone.

3 **Turn your key chain into** an adventure totem, to ignite your adventurous spirit each time you feel it in your pocket. Use a small climber's caribeener. Use a souvenir from an adventurous place, or a piece of a karate black belt, to remind you that you can be a marital artist in any moment.

4 **Show your current adventure gear** in your house, as art. Look for an old mannequin at a thrift store, dress her with your scuba gear, and put her in the corner of your powder room. Hang your wind-surfing sails from the basement ceiling. Hang your skis on the garage wall in a nostalgic ski lodge "X." You spent $800 for those beautiful skis and only use them ten days each year. Why not enjoy them all of the time?

5 **Fill your life with adventure.** Most houses have a small ledge around the tops of the windows and doors. Dust off these little adventurous

nooks and crannies and line them with Rambo figurines slithering on their bellies, superheroes standing up for truth and justice, or spacemen conquering new worlds. For just a few dollars at your local toy store, you can get a bag of little army soldiers, gladiators, cowboys, or dinosaurs. Use them to create an adventurous fantasy all around the secret perimeter of your home. Let these characters muster your adventurous spirit the next time you need courage to telephone someone and ask him or her out on a date.

6 **Create a large open space** where you can go and think. Ideally, one room of your house would be completely empty, except for comfortable pillows and candles, where you could go to sit and reflect. But even in a crowded apartment, you can carve out a niche and make a small meditation area, even if you don't meditate. You'll find it useful to make a corner of peace in your hectic life, where you can go to find a new perspective. We have become so used to nonstop activity

every day that a simple visit to open space gives access to a wonderful adventure of inner discovery.

7 **Make your bathroom mirror** into a personal window of adventure. Glue little sailboats around the perimeter if you dream of sailing into the sunset. Drape a plastic Hawaiian lei around your medicine cabinet and go to the beach every morning, as you glance in the mirror fresh out of bed. With a grease pencil, draw the exterior of a European train and put your face in the window, looking out on the countryside. Draw the window of a cable car so you can see yourself riding to the top of the Alps. Or draw the cockpit of an old airplane, and see your face in the captain's seat, looking down the runway in preparation for takeoff.

8 **Invest in bathtub toys.** Recreate your childhood bath time. Buy rubber ducks, Mr. Bubble, and battery-powered submarines. Fill the tub,

close the door, and get lost in the secret world of your own bathtub.

9 **Bury a time capsule** in the wall of your house. Load it with items that matter to you, such as an article from the daily newspaper, a picture of yourself, something you've made or written, and anything else that you would want to send to a future generation. Enjoy assembling a package of things that you would just as readily send into outer space to tell aliens who you really are. Do this next time you are bored on a rainy day. Relish the process of summarizing your existence with a small box of memories. Enjoy the adventure of imagining who will discover your treasures.

10 **Buy adventurous pajamas,** with or without feet. Find a rocket ship or fairytale pattern that reminds you of the adventures you had as a child. Go to sleep in them, prepared to have adventurous dreams.

11 **Hang a prism** above a window to break up the light into a rainbow spectrum. It will give your room new energy and each spot of color will remind you that everyday life can be broken into an infinite number of adventures.

12 **Remove rejection** from your home. Somewhere in your house you have saved all your rejection notices for your novel, the Dear John letters from ex-lovers, termination letters from work, and nasty notes from your ex-spouse. That energy keeps you from being fully available for new adventures that come your way. Explorers on the new frontier don't dwell on past failures. Get all these negative drains out of your home.

13 **Don't keep anything** you don't feel good about. When your house is filled with items you don't really want, you stifle your adventurous freedom. Get rid of everything you have in your house that is there

because of an obligation. You don't have to eat on dishes you hate just because they were a gift from your in-laws. Sell them at a garage sale. Give them away. And get plates that make you feel good about sitting down in your home for a warm meal. If you receive a gift, you have no obligation to like or keep it; otherwise, it's not a gift! Surround yourself exclusively with items you love.

14 **Build a slot-car track,** a multi-level train set, a giant dollhouse, a loom, or a harpsichord. Inside every home, there should be a detailed, participatory, and adventurous world (other than satellite TV or the Internet) in which the homeowner can get lost.

15 **Collect something you love** and display it as art in your home...stamped-metal lunch boxes, PEZ dispensers, Matchbox cars, Trolls, salt shakers, Elvis memorabilia, rare books, or plates commemorating every state in America...whatever excites you can be

found on eBay or in a local novelty store. Find something that really makes you smile and enjoy the exciting hunt, as you seek to expand your collection. Prominently display your trophies in a glass showcase in your home.

16 **Display pictures** of your past adventures on the walls of your home. Display artifacts brought back from your travels. You may have only spent one week at Macchu Pichu, but make sure there is some evidence of your trip on display, to transport you back during the other fifty-one weeks of the year.

17 **Make a small altar** to your achievements. Display all your old trophies, diplomas, and plaques as well as pictures of yourself living your dreams. Make your accomplishments visible and you'll feel completely supported when you take new courageous actions. You may never get the acknowledgment you feel you deserve unless you give it to yourself. For most people, to bathe in acknowledgment is a completely unfamiliar experience and an adventure of exploration into the unknown.

18 **Create a space** that represents your own personal den. It could be a workshop, a fabric room, a deluxe kitchen, or a well-lit and heated garage. Make that space your little kingdom. Decorate it accordingly so it feels like your cave or your nest. Hang signs that will remind you as you walk in, e.g., "Bob's Workshop" or "Betty's Kitchen." Make certain that there is at least one space on your property that is reserved exclusively for you.

19 **Create themed adventures** in every room of your house, so that a walk through your home is like an adventure in Wonderland. Polish all the doorknobs, switch plates, drawers, and closet pulls to make a shiny room. Make one room monochromatic, decorated exclusively with blue. Paint the walls, floor,

and ceiling in one room with six of your favorite colors. Make a tiger room with striped wallpaper, pillows, and rugs. And a fish room with fish paintings and a giant fish tank. Or paint an assortment of songbirds in a *trompe l'oeil* forest. Fill your bird room with live parrots or hang a hummingbird feeder outside the window. Give each room a fantasy theme and create your own personal Disneyland, where anything is possible.

20 Use color to make your house more adventurous. Paint arches over your doorways and checkered patterns on your bland linoleum floors. Choose your favorite color for your exterior trim and a contrasting tone for your deck. Paint an old wooden chair (or be adventurous with fabric paint on an upholstered one), your bland kitchen cabinets, and the legs of your couch. Paint your hallway purple, paint one wall orange in a white room, paint your ceiling a bright color, paint all your doors turquoise or red. Color makes every part of your house a magical surprise.

21 **Give each appliance a name** and a personality. Give your vacuum a face and a cape. Paint your TV royal blue and your microwave yellow. Explore artistic ways to customize your generic black plastic appliances. How about stickers? Refrigerator magnets? Everyday items can either fall into the background of your boring life or come forward as starring partners in your adventurous home.

22 **Make your home more exciting** with fabric. Look for interesting pieces at yard sales and thrift stores. Drape dazzling prints over side tables and railings. Cover old armchairs and pillows with daring colors. Hang rayon sheets in doorways to form translucent screens between rooms. Hang antique clothing and sarongs on your walls as art. Display a series of adventurous hats, like leather flight helmets, pith helmets, or velvet top hats. Transform your boring flat white walls into an unpredictable and exciting array of colorful patterns and three-dimensional objects. Make a tour of your

home a memorable adventure for your next visitor. Your surroundings will make you feel more adventurous, too.

23 **Discover your ceilings.** Decorate them with flags, tapestries, and a universe of glow-in-the-dark constellations. Stop thinking within four walls. At your local model-airplane club, you might find someone who will give you a no-longer-flyable airplane for free that will look really impressive hanging from your rafters.

24 **Open your shades** and clean your windows to let the adventurous outdoors come inside. Remove your window screens in the winter; otherwise they will filter out adventures happening right outside your home. Leave the window open a crack so you can hear the birds. Install skylights. Replace your drafty old windows with larger, more efficient ones. Cut new windows in dark claustrophobic rooms. Shift your focus from

inside your home to outside. As more of nature's sights and sounds flood into your home, adventure will become a bigger part of your daily reality. Make your home more like a tent on a mountaintop than an insulated fortress.

25 Get the best carpet you can afford. Regardless of the overall quality of your neighborhood or property, the soles of your bare feet will transport you to the throne of your castle where you can imagine being king or queen on a medieval adventure. Use ample padding and you'll also evoke the memory of sensuous sand caressing your toes as you walk on a beautiful beach.

26 Put a globe or map of the world in your house. Paint a map of the world on your kitchen floor. Get a world-map shower curtain to remind you how much exploration you can really do in your lifetime. Your neighborhood is also on that globe; explore it with enthusiasm today.

27 **Invest heavily** in tools that help you do what you love. Equip your kitchen with stainless-steel gadgetry. You may not get to use your Leatherman and GPS very often, but make sure that your garlic peeler, toaster, and can opener are just as exciting to use, because of their innovative designs. Buy high-quality rakes, shovels, and trowels, to facilitate your personal adventurous afternoon in the garden, or beautiful fountain pens, if writing is your passion.

28 **Buy refrigerator magnets** and decorate your fridge with every destination and adventure you have ever wanted to take. Every trip to get a glass of milk should remind you of what's possible out in the world. Subscribe to adventure magazines. Tear out any pages that inspire you and post them in plain view as part of your adventurous refrigerator display.

29 **Go on a survival mission** in your own kitchen. Eat your way through your pantry and your freezer and don't buy any more food until you exhaust everything that you squirreled away in your home. On this archaeological dig, you'll be surprised to discover canned goods in old-fashioned packages and strains of mold you didn't know you could grow.

30 **Go on a cooking adventure.** Invest in varied ethnic cookbooks and make an adventurous new meal. Or make something completely from scratch. Hull your own rice or make your own pasta. Learn to bake bread. Make your own maple syrup.

31 **Eat in every room of your house.** Don't just eat at the kitchen table. Go on a picnic in your own home. Lay out a blanket and eat on the floor. Serve dinner to your spouse in the bathtub, or on the front steps, and see if the food tastes different.

32 **Make your own plates** and cups. Make your own clay mugs at your local craft center, and no two cups of tea will ever feel the quite the same.

33 **Leave your mail in the mailbox** for an entire week. Then, schedule an hour on Saturday morning to go through all of it, with the excitement that you would normally feel after returning from a week-long vacation. Handle each piece only once; pay the bills immediately, put all the junk mail immediately into the recycling bin, schedule upcoming events on your calendar, and discard out-of-date invitations and announcements. Conquer your mail before it floods your house.

34 **Hire someone to clean** your home, do your dishes, and do your laundry. People complain about insufficient time for adventure. Why waste time doing things you can easily outsource for a small fee? Hire a neighborhood kid to clean your kitchen every night to give you more time to cook an adventurous meal.

35 **Watch what flows** in and out of your house. Seek a net loss every day, whereby more flows out than in, such that you can discover the joyous practice of simplifying. Take home only what you really need. Carefully monitor the scraps of paper you bring into your life, like coupons, free newspapers, and little notes you write to yourself. Notice how you rarely refer back to such papers, even if you could find them! This new consciousness is an ongoing exploration, as you improve your skills to absorb in your mind what you really need. You'll start to celebrate returning home empty-handed and thus you can leave your adventurous home unobstructed with clutter.

36 Give your cat her own submarine.

When I was seven, I'd spend hours in a cardboard submarine, pretending to navigate around my room. It was little more than a cardboard box with torpedo tubes and a periscope, but it was the most adventurous place in my home. Make your cat a fortress or fortified bunker out of a well-decorated cardboard box. Let her remind you that you can go anywhere you want today. Or put a camouflage cape on your dog and take him for a walk to look for adventure.

37 Invest time and energy into the creation of an adventurous exercise space in your house. Too many people throw their free weights in the moldy basement. No wonder they never feel like working out. Put the exercise equipment in the nicest room in your house so that you can look out your favorite window while you sweat. Line the attic ceiling with rock-climbing holds so you can have fun while you build your strength. Don't get a wind trainer for your bike, get

rollers instead, where you actually ride your bike even though you remain stationary. It takes more concentration and it's much more exciting.

38 Fill your home with music. Don't just turn up the stereo in the living room. Put additional speakers around your house. Music can transport you far away from the stresses of your day. Install a small stereo in the kitchen and see what type of music makes cooking most fun. Put a small waterproof radio in your shower; no two showers will ever be the same. Turn up your favorite music and sing along at the top of your lungs, like your favorite rock star.

39 Journey to faraway places by simply flipping your light switch. Have a romantic meal in a Parisian café by dimming the lights in your dining room. Fill your basement with colored neon tubes to evoke a roadhouse far from the nearest interstate. String

white Christmas icicle lights along the banister of your main staircase to create the feeling of ascending the castle stairs in *Beauty and the Beast*. Fill your master bedroom with at least fifty candles and create the mood of a sacred cave in the Far East. Put blue bulbs in your powder room, so that a simple trip to the bathroom is fun and memorable for your guests.

40 **Cover all of your clocks** on Friday night and go on a timeless adventure. Enjoy the freedom for an entire weekend, with no commitments and no schedule. Listen to the rhythms of your body; eat when you are hungry, sleep when you are tired. Have a friend call you on Sunday night, so you can uncover the clocks and be on time for work.

41 **Get an adventure watch** with a compass, thermometer, and altimeter. Even if you just use it to figure out the elevation changes from the ground floor up to your office, it will always remind you that it's time for an everyday adventure.

42 Experiment with different plants.

Grow orchids. Set up a grove of cacti. Grow your own vegetables and herbs. A garden is a nonstop adventure; you never know what will come up. If you've closed off this option because you think you don't have a "green thumb," try again. At your local nursery, ask for detailed instructions to maximize your chances of keeping your new plants alive. Or get a book on plant care from the library.

43 Patronize Army surplus stores.

Your closet should house at least an adventurous antique leather flight jacket or a pair of Royal Air Force wool flying pants. Or put a "Keep 'em flying!" stick pin on your sport coat. Search eBay for a surplus fighter-jet ejection seat to put in your living room. Or buy a full-size commando mannequin and put him on a bench in your foyer, in full, adventure-ready garb.

44 **Create an adventure closet.** Fill it with your assorted gear. Even if you're consumed by work and rarely use the contents, just walking past your adventure closet might make you feel more comfortable, since you know what lives inside. You'll sleep better at night, knowing that you can open that door at any time.

45 **Set up** an air-pistol range in your basement. Pad the wall with an old mattress and buy a target trap at the sporting-goods store, to stop pellets from hitting your walls. Put an archery range in your yard, again with proper protection behind the target. Put a dartboard somewhere in your house. These are not for self-defense but for a novel release of the tension you develop at work and for the pursuit of a perfect bull's-eye.

46 **Buy adventurous furniture.** When you sleep on a waterbed, sleeping is never dull. Work at your grandfather's desk and imagine what his life was like when he was your age. Make your own dining-room table, and even a bad meal will still be a celebration. Stop buying furniture that solely gets the job done. Seek to fill your home with furniture that is full of personality and excitement. Your favorite chair may not be available at the mall; look for it on the side of the road instead. Once you spray-paint it metallic bronze, you'll have a chair you love and an adventurous story to go with it.

47 **Rearrange your furniture.** See whether moving your desk improves your concentration, or whether shifting your bed to the other side of the room helps you sleep better. Go on a detailed exploration of how your furniture is configured in your home and dare to move it to an unimaginable place. Discover the differences such subtle changes can make in your life.

48 **Bury your own treasure.** Wine cellars are not just reserved for wine drinkers. Build an inventory of something you love and store it all in one place. This is not about stocking up for an emergency. Instead, create a pile of treasure in your own home, so you can feel like your house is the keeper of an Indiana Jones–like tomb. Put a spotlight on the shipping pallet in your basement full of laundry detergent or ginger ale, if these are the products that excite you, and take pride in knowing that you have an unlimited supply.

OUTDOORS

49 **Make a secret paradise** in your backyard. Stack up rocks to form unique sculptures. Make a Buddha out of stones in your yard. Configure gnarled sticks around the perimeter of your property. Make your own koi or goldfish pond. Put in a small pump to make a cascading falls, to create your own peaceful water garden, where you can escape without leaving your property. Build a tree house. Clear a small trail to a private hideaway and put a bench or a glider there, so you can go on a mini vacation out to that quiet spot. If your property is wide open, you can create your little enclave out of latticework. Cover it with vines to make your secret spot more intimate.

50 Create magic spaces in public parks, if you have no yard. Use fallen tree limbs, stones, and dead plants. Make your own stone circle that's so beautiful, park officials will leave it intact for archaeologists to unearth thousands of years from now. Make a small stone-and-stick castle in a public park, similar to one you would make from sand at the beach. City officials may take it down, but you won't have to worry about it being digested by the sea at high tide.

51 Decorate your yard with a spirit of adventure. Hang a tire from a tree to make a swing. Hang an old life preserver on your back porch, even if you're landlocked. Stack your woodpile into a maze for your kids to explore, or so that it contains your initials, configured out of logs turned sideways. Carve your shrubs into topiary. Put an inflatable boat in the backyard, especially if you live in the desert, to remind you of floating in the ocean. A walk around your property should be an adventure, like in your own theme park, or on your own personal miniature golf course.

52 Make your front lawn an invitation to play. Line your walkway with old pedal toys that evoke a childlike memory of freedom. Install wickets for croquet or hoops for Frisbee golf. Make a piece of your yard into a mini putting green, a sandpit for horseshoes, or a boccie court, and your home will be an invitation for the neighborhood to come and play.

53 Look for discarded adventure gear and convert it into something fun. Search flea markets for a retired bumper car to put on your porch or for a single chair from a chairlift of a bankrupt ski area, to hang from a tree in your yard. Put a scarecrow on an old surfboard and hang it from a tree. Buy a $10 bike at a yard sale, cover the wheels with colorful fabric, and make it into a weathervane on the roof of your house. Make a retired Sunfish sailboat into a bench in your backyard. If you can't sit on the deck under sail on a gorgeous lake, at least you can enjoy the calm waters of your backyard. You can even fill the cockpit with ice and store cold drinks there when you have your next party.

54 Get a trampoline. Adventure often includes instability. A good jumping session completely shakes up your perspective and loosens up your adventurous spirit.

55 Become a beekeeper. Put hives on your property and collect your own honey. Adopt

local raccoons. Put a salt lick out for deer, and a birdbath for birds. Mount colorful birdhouses throughout your yard. Adopt your local critters. Learn about their adventurous world.

56 Make your mailbox into a signpost that says "Adventure lives here." Cut an old canoe in half and mount it on a pole at the end of your driveway, with your house number on the bow. Or visit a ski shop and ask them to save you at least two pairs of broken or discarded skis. Drive them into the ground at the end of your driveway in two Xs and lay your mailbox between them. Or ask a bike shop to save a bike with a broken frame that would otherwise be discarded. Secure a mailbox to the handlebars and lock the bike to a tree in front of your house. Give your generic galvanized steel mailbox an adventurous home.

57 **Surround your home** with adventurous mascots. Look for old stuffed animals at thrift stores and garage sales. Make them each their own parachute, with a piece of an old bed-sheet and some string, and hang them from the trees in your front yard. Make it appear that a squadron of furry paratroopers is invading your property for fun and adventure. Or dress your pink-flamingo lawn ornaments in adventurous garb.

58 **Get up on your roof.** Rig a rope for safety and climb to the highest point of your house, just to enjoy the view. Mount a flagpole at the summit, and fly your favorite flag to commemorate your first ascent. Or tie a rope to the baluster at the top of the highest stairs in your house and mount a small flag there. Periodically pull yourself up from the ground floor.

59 **Install an anemometer** on your roof, wind chimes on your porch, and a barometer in your living room. Make your home an adventurous weather station. Learn to follow the weather as it tracks through your neighborhood. Even though you may not travel as much as you would like, learn to watch the highs and lows track across the country. Follow each weather system on its adventure across America.

60 Sleep in a tent in your backyard. Rent one at the local camping store and spend a Saturday night sleeping in your yard with your spouse. Or leave your tent set up and sleep in it during a rainstorm, and get lost in the meditative drone of the storm.

61 Explore the night sky. Look in the paper for meteor-shower schedules. Build a hot tub outside and soak while you contemplate adventures in other galaxies. Put a telescope in your study and wonder if we are alone.

NOT JUST ANY PARKING SPACE

62 **Your adventurous home** starts in your parking space. Back your car into your driveway so you are ready to launch on your next adventure. Make a pathway of large stones from your parking space to your front door and leap from one to the other, as though you were rock hopping up a wild river in New Zealand. Or tie a rope to a tree and swing like Tarzan from your car to your doorstep. Install your own personal zip line. Coming home should be fun. Design your reentry so that it feels like an adventurous celebration.

63 **Decorate your garage** with adventurous abandon. Stop thinking of it as a moldy extra room in which you throw your mower and your recyclables. Make it into your own personal mission control. Display astronaut memorabilia. Hang Saturn V rockets from the ceiling. Rig a tape recorder to say, "The Eagle has landed," each time you enter. Or paint the entire space in mod flower-power colors, including giant pink and orange flowers on the floor, and park your VW Bug in a perfect little nest every night. At the very least, decorate the walls with themed posters or artwork, to make your garage part of your life instead of a space you just happen to pass through on your way to your car.

64 Make the mundane fun. Many people hang a tennis ball to hit their windshield or put a block in front of their tire to stop them from pulling too far into the garage. But where's the adventure in that? Hang a GI Joe paratrooper from the ceiling of your garage and pull in until he presses his adventurous cheek up against your windshield, to welcome you back to base.

65 Get a car that soars like your own personal biplane, waiting to take you for a barnstorming adventure. Look in the used-car classifieds (*Hemmings Motor News* is one of the largest) to find the classic car of your dreams. Or buy any convertible. When you put the top down on a full-moon night, the entire sky is yours in which to fly.

66 **Get a motorcycle.** No errand is ever dull when you go on your motorcycle. Or get a Vespa scooter, put on your beret, and pick up a baguette at the local bakery. Get a new bicycle with baskets, and run your errands on that. On two wheels, you might just discover something on your way to the store that you have driven past one thousand times before.

67 **Personalize the inside of your car.** Make your car an expression of your personality, like your own personalized backpack or pocket book. Buy assorted storage bins to organize self-help cassettes and foods to satisfy all of your moods. Keep enough CDs on hand so that each drive can have its own sound-track. Paste a picture of your favorite celebrity on the driver's-side backseat window (where it won't block your view of traffic) and make it look like you are taking them for a ride. Make your own hood ornament. Affix your favorite character to your dashboard. Hang an Indiana Jones figurine from your rearview mirror.

68 **Make the outside** of your car unique. No two Toyotas or Hondas have to be the same. Affix bumper stickers that express your point of view, paint zebra stripes, and give your car steer horns or paper-mache wings. At the very least, get a license-plate frame that says something about your adventurous spirit.

HOME IS HOW IT SUITS YOU

Every home is a new adventure. I used to live in a three-bedroom condo with lots of closets, a garage, and an entire attic full of stuff. When I got divorced, half of the stuff moved out. But I filled it up again when I hung giant remote-control gliders from the ceiling and put a slot-car track on the floor of my office. The walls were adorned with pictures and artifacts from my various adventures around the world.

Then I did something extreme. I moved out to live on a tandem bike in Europe with my girlfriend. I emptied most of the contents of the two thousand square foot condo into four dumpsters. I took ninety-four shirts and twelve pairs of shoes and donated them to Goodwill. I put some furniture and clothes in a 10x10x10 self-storage room and filled a van with enough junk to earn $400 from a yard sale.

On my bike I lived out of my saddlebags and luggage trailer for five months while coaching clients from the road. While this lifestyle is not for everyone, it was exceptionally refreshing to carry everything I needed on my bike for such a long time. Adventure was no longer something merely decorating the walls of my home; when I moved onto my bike, there were no longer any walls to my adventure. This compact existence made it particularly easy for me to fully experience the people and sights that flashed in front of me.

When I came back to Connecticut to write this book, I rode my bike around my favorite neighborhood and put three hundred flyers in mailboxes asking people to call me if they knew of an apartment to rent. I got a call from a wonderful family with a small apartment in their basement, and I rented it right away.

For many months I have lived in a place that is smaller than my former master bedroom. It happens to be one of the most wonderful places I've ever lived. It's just 15x13 feet with an attached kitchen (6x10) and bathroom. There's a Murphy bed built into the wall that looks like the captain's berth in a stateroom of a luxury yacht. There's one closet, one dresser, three lamps, one table, and two chairs. It has rough-hewn wood paneling; the knots and grain of the boards decorate all the walls. I'm forced to monitor everything I bring into my life, because there really isn't much room for anything that I don't need. And that's what makes it so incredibly refreshing. My stripped-down, simplified abode allows me to dedicate maximum attention to writing, coaching, and nature.

Outside my door, I have thousands of clouds and trees. My backyard is made up of a horse farm on one side and a nature preserve on the other, with a river running through it. The river plays the soundtrack for my backyard and it's overlaid with the sounds of songbirds and neighing horses. Would I have been so aware of these glorious surroundings if I had three bedrooms here to manage or if I owned this property? As a renter, I have the freedom to completely enjoy living here without the worries of maintaining it.

The apartment keeps my bike trip alive for me. If I moved into a bigger place, the spirit of the bike trip might fade away and become something I longed for from my past. Instead, this home is actually a lot bigger than the saddlebags and trailer that used to hold my things. Thus, it is quite luxurious.

As I was sitting outside today and talking to a client on the phone, a red-tailed hawk dove down to make a kill, just barely thirty feet in front of my face. This is the ultimate reward for living this way. Anyone could have seen this hawk in his or her yard. But my home always keeps me focused outside where I am more apt to experience it.

My last three homes have taught me that a home is always an adventure. It's not something you're ever stuck with. You can create a conventional or unconventional experience. And no matter where you live or where you are in your life, you can always make it fit you like a glove.

the
adventure
of
relationships

Every relationship in your life is a potential adventure. Wonderful, fascinating, interesting people pass through your life. Your day is filled with glorious people, everywhere around you, each with their own fascinating story to tell. Is there someone really interesting hiding inside that unassuming package? Does that gorgeous person you keep noticing really have anything to say? What are people thinking as they flow past you? Are they thinking the same things as you? Wouldn't it be fun to find out?

While you're focused on your "to do" list, other people with their own lists sometimes pass within inches. Unless you engage them, they disappear into the ether. Every near miss is an adventure waiting to happen. Practice bridging the gap between two goal-focused people. Fill that space so that adventure can occur.

Engage the people around you simply for the sake of adding something new and novel to the mundane errands in your life. Look for simple ways to make contact.

Don't focus on getting people's phone numbers and going on dates, although that may end up being part of your relationship adventures. Concentrate on connecting with the people in your day. Make chance encounters happen. Relate to the people who pass through your life. This is a glorious piece of being alive that is yours to engage simply by smiling and opening your mouth.

Everyone that you meet represents an adventure waiting to happen. Practice adventurous relating at least once a day. Whether it's with your butcher or with your lover, challenge your assumptions and explore the depth of your connection. You have more in common with the people all around you than you think. And maybe they are hoping to be in deeper relationship with you, but they are too scared to initiate the dialogue. Be a courageous leader. This is one domain of your life where you never have to modulate your enthusiasm. Not all people will be willing to join you. But the more people you engage, the more likely you will surround yourself with a community of wonderful kindred spirits, ready to join you on your journey through life.

People are your ultimate resource for everything you need and want, whether it's love, a new job, or a squash partner. Relationship adventures are an ongoing opportunity for people to give and take with freedom, as part of the perfect flow of life. So practice being available for the relationship adventures all around you, and you might just find that, sooner or later, people will give you what you always dreamt was possible.

CLOSE TO HOME

We obsess about getting away from it all to a place where adventure really lives. We hope one day to have a country home or enough freedom to extend our vacation time. But there is so much adventure right in your neighborhood that you never need to leave, only to change your focus. Look for simple and rich opportunities right in your backyard. Let go of the notion that adventure only happens after a plane ride, and you'll settle into a blissful relationship with your local everyday life.

69 **Ride through your neighborhood** on your bike. Cruise your local roads, seeking adventure. Turn down all the dead-end streets. Leave your spandex at home; this is not an aerobic exercise ride. There is an interesting house in your neighborhood with old cars that you love, an unusual sculpture on the front lawn, beautiful custom windows, or a marvelous flowering tree. Share your compliment to the owner out on the front lawn. Or ring the bell. Compliment them on what you noticed. Chances are good that they will be flattered that you noticed their unusual wind chimes or collection of shorthaired cats. And they may become a friend for life.

70 **Visit yard sales.** Homeowners are usually very relaxed and happy when they are collecting money for their junk from the comfort of their own front lawn. This is a precious time to meet the people in your neighborhood. You'll find people very approachable, whether you buy something or not.

71 **Participate fully** in the things you love at a local level. The people you want to meet are waiting for you at the places you love to go, as long as you remain open to meeting them. Be available for relationship adventures at the beach, on the path you jog after work, or in your yoga class. This week, join a club of like-minded individuals. Sign up for a course in spirituality. Make one night a week available for doing something you love in the company of others. You'll find the best relationship adventures here—maybe even romance.

72 **Don't ignore an opportunity** to be neighborly, because it's really an opportunity for an adventure. For example, if you notice that someone has left their headlights on, ring the bell to let them know. Start a search party for a lost pet. Call for help if a tree is down in a storm, or a burglar alarm is going off. Get involved—the reward for you will be connections you never would have made otherwise.

73

Look for new people to meet in the first ten minutes after you leave your house. Say hello to the parking-lot attendants and people standing next to you on the platform before your train arrives. Introduce yourself to the person sitting next to you on the train. Offer to share a taxi with a stranger also waiting for a cab. Don't just say hello and run off; pause after your greeting to see if maybe there is something between the two of you that needs to unfold. Be courageous. Introduce yourself to everyone you encounter. You only need to be confident about your name and your occupation, which is usually enough fuel to start a relationship adventure, as long as the other person is available.

74

Talk to overnight couriers. There are real people driving those vans. Ask them what's the funniest thing they have ever seen while attempting a delivery. Ask them what they like to do on their weekends. Get to know the person behind the uniform.

75 **Borrow someone's dog** and walk it in a park. With the dog on a leash, let him or her lead you to a neighborhood adventure.

76 **If you want to meet new people,** arrive at all your appointments fifteen minutes early. You'll be amazed by how much time you suddenly have to explore adventure with new friends you meet in the waiting room.

77 **Engage your neighbors.** Pay them a visit. Return everything you borrowed. Stop and talk to people you would normally pass by. Share something about yourself with the people you meet.

78 **Ask an elderly neighbor** to tell you stories about how the neighborhood used to look.

79 Help a neighborhood kid fix his bike or study French. If he shows interest, teach him something you know how to do.

80 Lead a nature walk for your community. You'll meet other residents who care about nature. Once you commit to such an event, you'll also hone your knowledge of the nature in your neighborhood and discover new species of flora, and maybe even fauna, you never knew existed.

81 Organize an event to save a local estate or clean up a local river. Take a stand in your community for a cause that moves you. People will see the leader in you and they will be attracted to make your acquaintance.

82 Stop at every lemonade stand. Any child in front of a house with a sign is an opportunity to reminisce about your own childhood. It's also an opportunity to stop and meet more people who live in your town.

83 **Offer assistance** when you see someone stuck on the side of the road. You'll make new friends and genuinely provide much-needed support.

84 **Be visible in your neighborhood.** Walk, Rollerblade, skateboard, unicycle, or jog around your block on a daily basis, or at least several times each week. Allow enough time so that you can stop to meet the people who live on your journey.

85 **Memorize** the small details on your route. Small changes will become more exciting, and you'll notice little adventures unfolding before your eyes. Perhaps one neighbor got a new car. Or a new baby came home. Or a peregrine falcon killed a pigeon and left the carcass in the parking lot. Or a new gravestone was placed in the local cemetery. Make time to notice the details in the lives of the people in your neighborhood. Each detail is an invitation for a relationship adventure.

86 Engage some of the details you see. Bring a wildflower to the house with the new baby. Offer condolences for a death in the family. Admire someone's new car. Step into the lives of the people who live in your backyard—not in a nosy or gossipy way, but to simply marvel at your connection with the people around you that you have taken for granted for too long.

87 Pause to savor. Bring a lawn chair across the street from your house and look back at the life you created. Invite your neighbors across the street to be part of your adventure. Sit with them, looking at your house or apartment building and front lawn from their yard. Invite them over to sit on your property and look back on their home. Look back at your life in your neighbors' eyes. Take a picture of your home and post it on your refrigerator so you can always appreciate the life you have built.

88 **Go out on your lawn** or set a lawn chair on the sidewalk in front of your apartment building to paint, write, or make art in public. Put yourself in the flow of people streaming past your front door. Set up your own sidewalk café. Leave an empty chair at the table while you make a collage or draw; you never know who will stop by. Make it even more enticing for someone to join you on your adventure…put a pitcher of your favorite beverage on the table and an empty glass at the empty seat.

89 **Be authentic** with your neighbors. Share what you love. Confess that you collect Beatles memorabilia or that organizing complex problems pleases you. When you meet people in your hometown, strive to share your authentic passion without expectation of a result. You might just meet someone who wants to be a partner on your antique-hunting adventures.

90 **Talk to people** walking their dogs. Admire their pets. They will be delighted to speak with you about their animal. And you never know where the conversation will lead.

91 **Take a leadership role** in a local club.

92 **When you show up** for an event and discover it's canceled, don't just turn around and drive home mad. You immediately have something in common with everyone else who shows up and discovers that plans have changed. Make your own event with other frustrated attendees. Go to lunch together. Hold your own concert, class, or lecture with the talent that you have available. Be available to turn a frustrating evening into a luscious adventure, even though your original plans have fallen apart.

93 How ya doin'? Practice greeting the people in your path and actually listen to their response. Don't say, "How are you?" without really meaning it and listening for a real response. Don't say, "What's new?" without listening for something interesting. Respond to similar questions with genuine responses. Try greeting people with, "Hi, what's the most adventurous thing you've done in the last twenty-four hours?" Don't take simple greetings for granted. Be open to the adventures that may come up.

94 **Shake hands** or hug every person you meet in your neighborhood. Each one of the people in your town deserves a special greeting of human contact. Take an extra second to touch the people who live all around you.

RETAIL RELATIONSHIP ADVENTURES

Errands are often perceived as mundane components of life. Some people even hire a concierge to handle all these errands for them so that they can do "what really matters." But when everyday adventure becomes a priority, every errand is actually an opportunity for a great time. Even though shopping centers are often congested expanses of asphalt and concrete, they are also places where fellow adventurers go in search of what they need. Go shopping to meet new people and take home the items you purchase as a bonus. Look for the simplest little encounters on every trip to the store, and suddenly errands will start to seem like mini vacations instead of obligations.

Everyone in your path is either a stranger or a potential co-adventurer. You get to make the call, and either way you're right. But why not look for adventure on your trip to the supermarket, bank, or gas station? Even if you made an annual trip to scale Mt. Everest, you'd still probably spend more total hours every year in the aisles of the supersaver mart. So make it your own personal Everest. Mount an expedition on every trip and look for wonderful new people to fill up your life with fun and excitement.

95 Take the backroads. Don't just jump on the highway and take the quickest route to the mall. Go through a nearby small town and stop at that little family-owned bakery or ice cream shop on the way. You might even want to rummage through the thrift store on the edge of town, for buried treasure or for the very item you were going to buy at the mall.

96 **Admire the small businesses** in your nearest shopping center. Go on a tour. Sample each of the small shops, even if they sell something you would never use. Go in and introduce yourself, just for the experience of seeing a new business for the first time. Local shopkeepers are a great neighborhood resource. Ask lots of questions.

97 **Stop waiting** for other people to say hello first. Greet everyone in your path, with no attachment to whether he or she notices or not. This is not a popularity contest but merely an invitation. People can engage you or not with complete freedom. But when you open yourself up with a greeting, you invite adventure into your life.

98 **Go on adventures** with sales help. Don't just ask them if they have what you are looking for. Ask them about their experience with a product. I

went to the local housewares warehouse to buy a frying pan. I asked to speak to someone who cooks and spent twenty minutes with Keith learning about the virtues of cast iron, aluminum, and stainless steel. In the process, I got to know what he likes to cook and where he and his wife disagree in the kitchen. I never had so much fun buying such a mundane item.

99 Pay attention to name tags. Thank salespeople by name. Before you hang up on telemarketers, yell out their name. When you are on the phone with the bank, credit-card company, or airlines, call the operator by name. Each time you say someone's name back to them, you are launching a relationship adventure because you stand out. Most other callers fail to acknowledge that there is a live person at the other end of the phone. This simple practice makes these boring and often frustrating calls into an adventure, where anything becomes possible.

100 Acknowledge the cashier. When
you fixate solely on the product you place on the checkout counter, you bypass the rich adventure possible with the human being who collects your money. Look them in the eye. Smile. Share something about your purchase. For example, "I need this shirt for an interview tomorrow. I hope I get the job." A comment like this can make the difference between an impersonal shopping experience and little relationship adventure.

101 Don't shy away from people you
think you recognize, even if you haven't seen them for some time. When someone who looks familiar comes down the aisle of the supermarket, rather than hiding in the laundry detergent aisle, say hello and explore what might have changed in the years since you saw one another last.

102 **Dive into conversation** with super-market shopping-cart drivers who look interesting. Offer a simple hello when you pass them in the aisle. Nothing more is needed. Surrender all attachment to any outcome. Just be free. You'll discover that people will turn and ask why you look so familiar or if you are a celebrity. People will feel invited to engage you on the adventure of being alive. You'll leave the supermarket with more than just groceries for the first time...you'll ride home with a pocket full of phone numbers for new friends and business contacts, and maybe even a date.

103 **Step outside** the norm and ask strangers questions about produce. Which is better, kale or collard greens? Are pink grapefruits sweeter than the yellow ones? Ask everyone, from potential lovers to senior citizens, just for the fun of watching people speak passionately about their favorite foods. When someone makes you smile because they shared a family secret for distinguishing the ripest pineapple, relish the adventure

you just had. Someone just got passionate about a piece of fruit, simply because you asked a question in the otherwise boring produce aisle.

104 **Hold the door** for someone at the ice cream freezer case. Ask them if they have ever tried your favorite flavor. Find out which vanilla they think is creamiest. Share an ice cream with a fascinating stranger, even if you both do nothing more than put the same flavor into your carts.

105 **Try a new breakfast cereal.** As you survey the huge supermarket cereal aisle, ask the next person who passes which brand they prefer and take at least one new cereal home with you. The next morning, savor every bite. You were adventurous and welcomed a stranger to your breakfast table, even though you may never see that person again.

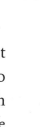

106 **Let out your inhibitions** in the supermarket. Try to make other shoppers laugh. Get excited about a new brand of laundry detergent. Make recommendations to fellow shoppers you see struggling with the thousands of choices in every aisle. Encourage someone to take home something new.

107 **Talk to people** in supermarket checkout lines. I like to let people with few items go ahead of me when I have a cart full of groceries, which immediately facilitates a conversation. Ask them if those fruit-juice-sweetened cookies in their cart taste good. Tell them you wanted to make sure they could get their shrimp home promptly to get it in the refrigerator. Be spontaneous and you'll find yourself on a relationship adventure.

108 **Give a gift** each time you leave the supermarket. Instead of abandoning your shopping cart in the parking lot, wheel it back to the entrance and give it to the next customer, for the sheer adventure of making contact with another shopper just like yourself.

109 **The next time you get gas**, talk to the person filling up next to you. If you are at a highway rest area, ask them where they are going, or where they are coming from. Admire their car. Complement them on how clean it looks. Ask them if they like their new Accord as much as you like your Camry. Make your fill-up something more than a boring chore.

110 **Allow ten extra minutes** to pick up the dry cleaning or visit your shoe repairman. Talk to your service people for a few minutes. Ask how they are doing, what's new, how's business. Get to know the people who work on the components of your life.

111 **Meet chronically late people** at a restaurant so that you can get to know the waiters and waitresses while you wait. Initiate a relationship adventure with the people sitting next to you. Savor the time you have to meet someone new rather than wasting time being mad that your friend is late once again. When someone shows up late, they actually give you an adventurous gift.

112 **Make magic** while you stand in line. Talk to the people behind and in front of you. When you wait in line for a movie, ask the people near you if they read any reviews of the film you are about to see. You might just meet someone who will change your life. And even if you don't, you can have a lot of fun just joking with other people in line.

113 Talk to people when you go to public restrooms. The bathroom is a great equalizer, where each of you has let down your guard. Perhaps that person holding the door is a prospective friend or client. Be friendly. Comment on the movie you both just saw or your favorite food at the restaurant where you're both dining. You never know what adventures might ensue.

FRIENDS

Deepen your connections with the people you've chosen to be a recurring part of your life. Don't just share activities with your friends. Share your feelings, too, at the deepest level. Be more intimate. Let them see more of you and they will reward you with the same. As you shed your skin, an unfamiliar and exciting new layer will be exposed.

Every friendship is full of adventure waiting to happen. View your friendships as open doorways into adventurous places. A world of possibilities exists with your friends; it's a world not available for you if you remain isolated and on your own. Your friends bring with them their own adventurous definitions and experiences. Ask them to share their world with you; you'll both deepen your friendship as a result.

114 **Make storytelling important** to your friendships and you'll discover a new way to deepen your connections. Explore what's concealed beneath the surface of your friendships. Ask your friends to share previously unrevealed stories from their past and dreams for their future. Sit on the edge of your seat as you listen, with the same excitement you'd bring to an adventurous movie. Everyone has a rich story to tell about their past and dreams they keep hidden. Explore what's concealed beneath the surface of your friendships.

115 **Share your complaints** directly with your friends instead of complaining behind their backs. Tell them exactly what's missing in your friendship. Ask them what they need from you. If nothing changes to your satisfaction, either let go of your complaints or seek new friends. Either way, get out of the lifeless middle ground where complaints abound. Be courageous and discover a new standard for honesty in all your friendships. Blaze a trail outside the boundaries you normally establish for your friendships.

116 **Open up a new frontier** where anything can be said and any emotion can be expressed and you'll take each friendship on an adventure. Say no to a friend who is asking too much from you. Reveal your undeclared expectations of your friends. Tell them how to listen to you. Perhaps you just want to be heard, with no feedback. Or maybe you want them to give you the answer that you know lives in your blind spot. Ask your friends what they expect of you. Ask for the freedom to get angry with your friends, all as part of a new domain of adventurous friendship.

117 **Pick up new friends** who share your interests. Chase down another mountain biker on the trail, just to say hello. You might find yourself training and racing with that new friend next year. Speak to that person you always see on Sundays at the garden center. Say hello to that person at the coffee bar who always has a stack of books you'd like to read. We tend to think that "picking people up" is reserved for singles in bars, where the risk of ego-destroying rejection is terrifying. But when you are doing what you love, talking to strangers holds little threat. Even if they reject you, you are still out enjoying what you love! Go after people who look like they have a common interest.

118 **Empower your friends** to be part of your support team on all your adventures. Tell a friend to call or email once a week to remind you beforehand not to betray yourself at work. Ask a friend to remind you not to be reactive when you meet your parents. Request that friends remind you of your greatest attribute on a regular basis and see if that keeps you from lapsing into periods of self-doubt. Tell your friends how to provide a parachute as you dive into your adventurous daily life.

119 **Declare one of your friends** your best friend. By naming the relationship, you bring power and clarity to your friendship, and open up the possibility that you can both explore someplace new. Go for a walk at least once each week and take turns revealing secrets. Once you declare one best friend, you might discover that you want to give a few more the same designation! Challenge the limits of intimacy possible in your friendships.

120 **Play new games** with your friends. When you change the venue that is familiar in your friendships, you might be surprised to see that everyone becomes unrecognizable. Play charades or *Pictionary* with a group of friends you know from the rock climbing gym or ski club. A simple game can sometimes be an even bigger adventure than the thrill-seeking activities you normally share. Play capture the flag, softball, or ultimate Frisbee with friends from work. Meet at a large school field at night to play flashlight tag. Everyone hides in the shadows until the person with the light illuminates the next person, who is then "it." Even a group trip to the bowling alley or a miniature golf course can be adventurous, if it were something you wouldn't ordinarily do with your friends.

121 **Invite a friend** to join you on a trip to a place you always wanted to visit.

122 **Plan a party** with your friends to help you meet new people. Print invitations and pass them out to all the interesting people you see during your day, to whom you are afraid to speak, but hope to meet.

123 **Meet a large group** of friends for an inspirational movie and then discuss the film over dinner.

124 **Invite your friends** to an adventurous theme birthday party. Print some interesting questions on the invitation. Ask your friends what they learned in the last year. What was their biggest accomplishment? What was their biggest regret? Sit in a circle and talk about life. If you feel like some of your friends aren't normally very intimate, you might be surprised to see that they have a lot to share in a group discussion that you have set up in celebration of your birthday.

125 **Gather** with a group of friends around a campfire to toast marshmallows and make s'mores. Ask each person to bring the printed lyrics of his or her favorite song, so you can sing well into the night.

Find a fire pit next to a lake or hot spring, in which you can soak or swim under the full moon.

Relationships from the Past

Your past is a vast resource for relationship adventures. Strive for healthy relationships with people from your past so you can proceed with your life in peace. Look for opportunities to go back in time and say what you didn't have the skill to say at the time. It's never too late. Each time you contact people you haven't spoken to in years, you open a gateway to something new that you might not have imagined would be possible.

126 **Each week,** reconnect with at least one old friend. Call someone from your past just to see how he or she is doing and to tell him or her that you miss them. If you don't have a database or Rolodex full of old friends, start one today.

127 **Call at least one** former teacher every year and thank them for something they shared that is still with you. Acknowledge the contribution they made to your life. Start by calling your old elementary school to track down the music teacher who taught you to sing. Then call your high school shop teacher who taught you how to work with wood. Thank them for the skills that led to your singing career or cabinet-making business that gives you so much joy today.

128 **Find your college roommates** and say hello. Share a memory about the first time you met.

129 **Contact someone from your past** where a romance almost happened. Perhaps circumstances are now different and something new will occur. Or maybe you were all wrong; there never was a spark between you. Call that person and ask what was true. Even if you have no desire to reconnect, the phone call will leave you freed up to explore new relationships without this one lingering in the back of your mind.

130 Go on an adventure back to the place of your first kiss. Call your first crush and find out whatever happened to him or her. Or find out if that person is now available, so you can continue what you started so many years ago. Call your first lovers just to reminisce. Share your best memory of something wonderful that the other person may have long ago forgotten. Apologize for anything you still don't feel good about. You might discover that your former partner doesn't even remember something you were certain had been a big mistake in your past. Such conversations will leave you feeling free.

131 Organize a reunion. Plan a gathering of any group of old friends, ranging from

elementary-school pals to work buddies from a now defunct company. It's fascinating to observe how you all have (or haven't) changed.

132 **Travel back** to the places that part of you never left. You left a piece of yourself at your college that you have been beating yourself up for not completing and another piece at the company you quit. You had completely valid reasons at the time. Go back and rescue those pieces of yourself and come home whole.

133 **Bring your bike** to your old neighborhoods and roll around to see how things have changed. Find the first house you lived in after your birth, knock on the door, and ask to see your old room.

FAMILY

In our families, we often find the most stagnant relationships in our lives. Most people become resigned to the fact that the cast of characters is completely set in its ways, and all adventure therefore comes to an end. Bring a new adventurous spirit to these relationships and be a leader, as you initiate new levels of togetherness. The holidays are a great place to redouble your efforts, so that this year's gatherings include unprecedented sharing and intimacy, coupled with less reactivity, as each person runs their usual routine. Let them do what they always do while you simultaneously invite them to a brand-new place.

134 Make a photo album to commemorate little adventures that you've shared with your family. Showcase all the times your parents encouraged you to be adventurous and to try new things. Exhibit the album at your next family gathering and invite everyone in your family to contribute photos and mementos, or to make their own albums.

135 **Spend an adventurous lunch** with your parents and do something unprecedented, particularly if they have been driving you crazy. Ask them to teach you something, like how an internal combustion engine works or the difference between all the flowering trees in your neighborhood. Ask them to share the three most important lessons in their lives. They will be proud to share their expertise with you. Your invitation for them to contribute is one of the greatest gifts you can give and will take your relationship into uncharted territory.

136 **Make your birthday** an adventure for your parents. Call each one of them and thank them for bringing you into the world. Acknowledge them both for the specific traits they each gave you. Explain how those traits play a significant role in your adult life. You are a product of the teachings of each of them, even though they both may be very different from you. If they have passed away, write them each a letter that thanks them for what they have given you.

137 **Plan an annual gathering** for the entire family to come together. Schedule a reunion or a party for all generations. Organize a softball game for the entire family. See how many generations you can assemble for a Thanksgiving bash.

138 **Send someone** in your family on an adventure. Chip in with your siblings and send your parents on an adventurous trip. Or facilitate an intimate adventure for your kids. Give them a weekend-long vacation anywhere in the country, as long as they go together and without their families or spouses.

139 **Plan** a family dining adventure with your nuclear family intact. Exclude the various stepparents and half-siblings for just one meal. Sit at a table as the same family unit you grew up with, even if your parents divorced long ago. View a childhood meal through adult eyes on an adventure into your past.

140 **Pick your parents up in a limo** and take them to something they would love, just because they did such a great job raising you.

141 **Explore new territory** and go beyond where you would normally communicate with your parents. Talk to them about what they thought you would become or who they thought you would marry. Ask them about their childhoods and what their lives were like when they were your age. Ask them to reveal three pivotal moments in their lives and to describe what life was like when you were born. Surprise them and tell them the worst thing you did as a teenager. The statute of limitations has run out for whatever you did behind their backs. Share a secret with them just to see if they've known all along. Don't just confine your conversations with your parents to the same old thing. Take your relationship someplace new.

142 **Show up** at your next holiday meal wearing protection. Designate something in your closet as your kevlar and Gore-Tex anti-reactivity outfit, that's breathable but causes all familial abuse to bounce off. Wear it like Indiana Jones in a chamber full of asps. If you don't react, they won't bite you.

143 **Find an adventurous way** to criticize your parents. Hire a skywriter to tell them to stop picking on your posture. Put a classified ad in their paper to tell them it hurts your feelings when they keep saying you should have been a doctor. Put a note in their pants pocket or pocketbook that says, "Stop criticizing your son/daughter for X, Y, and/or Z. You only make them angry, which just pushes them further away." Try to write it in their handwriting, so they will find the scrap of paper and think that they came up with this wise statement on their own. At the very least, they'll smile at your ingenuity for delivering a message that they hadn't been able to hear when you said it out loud.

144 **Do something fun** with each of your parents individually. Go someplace way outside the box. Take them to an ethnic restaurant, a theatre performance with naked actors, or to a movie that will allow you to discuss the meaning of life. Or do with your father what he most loves to do, like skeet shooting or ice fishing, just because you want to be with him while he is doing what he loves.

145 **Call everyone** in your family in a single day, just to say hello.

146 **Call a distant relative** and reconnect. Visit a distant relative in a foreign country.

147 **Create something** really fun with your siblings. Rent a movie you remember watching together as kids and invite them over for a surprise. Edit all of your dad's old home movies onto a videocassette and watch images of your childhood, when you and your siblings enjoyed adventure on a daily basis. Plan a weekend away to a place where you used to play together as kids, to rekindle the adventurous spirit that used to be present in your relationship.

WITH YOUR LOVER

Make your sleeping companion your adventure companion. Schedule adventurous activities together. And be spontaneous. Give your partner a list of items to pack and take them on a mysterious adventure away for the weekend. Tell them what to wear for the date but don't tell them where you are going. A combination of planned and spontaneous adventures is an antidote for any stale romance or marriage.

Your relationship with your spouse or lover is a fertile ground for adventure, even though so many people complain that they can never get what they need from this relationship. It will initially take discipline to make your marriage or romance adventurous, because you may have given up on ever getting that feeling back. But with creativity, you'll discover that you can make your relationship extremely exciting.

148 **Surprise your lover** with at least one gift a month. The value is not important; some free wildflowers or a beautiful stone picked up at the beach will do just fine. But take the time to give something as a token of your passion for your partner. Such surprises add an element of excitement to your most intimate relationship. You become a detective, always searching for something wonderful and simple to give. Your partner never knows what you will bring home next.

149 **Do something** for your partner today that you have never done before. Put yourself in their shoes and do their regular errands and chores.

You'll give them a break and make a contribution. But you'll also have an adventure by experiencing someone else's world.

150 **Go to the place** where you and your partner had your first date to reminisce and discuss how your lives have changed.

151 **Stop expecting** your partner to share your interests. Do what you need to do and give your partner the option of joining you or not. Many people sacrifice their adventurous spirit because they are waiting for their partners to join in. Go on an adventure alone if you have to.

152 **Take your partner** someplace new, even if it's just a walk down a new street. Go on evening explorations, like a drive in the country or a hike along a beach, and surprise your partner with a picnic meal or a bottle of wine. Go together to unpredictable places. Try new ethnic restaurants. Shop at new stores. Go places you've never been before, just for the adventure of it.

153 Make something with your partner. Restore an old car together that both of you would like to drive. Build a garden in your backyard. Make a piece of furniture together that you will both enjoy in your home. Spend some time every weekend creating, constructing, or renovating something. Don't renovate or build an entire house together; that seems to overwhelm most couples. Choose a smaller project. Local continuing-education classes might be a place to start.

154 Make art with your partner. Paint together. Make jewelry together. Choose a twenty-minute project from a book of writing exercises and then read one another the results. Share creative space with your lover. Spend an evening together in your living room, each reading your own book. Or hang out in an art studio and make a collage while your partner ties flies.

155 **Commit to a film,** theatre, or opera series together. Many libraries and colleges offer regular themed films, often for free. Or buy a membership at a theatre that interests both of you and agree to at least a monthly outing, to enjoy art together. Make these outings nonnegotiable dates where the two of you can enjoy some time alone.

156 **Share an adventurous vacation** together. Search for a trip that delivers a quality experience regardless of your varying skill levels. Possibilities include rafting trips, hiking trips, horseback adventures, scuba trips, cruises, and safaris. But make

certain that you each have the opportunity to go at your own pace, otherwise one of you is going to have a miserable time. Most couples survive an adventure trip that has either physical challenges or uncomfortable living conditions. If you choose a trip with both, you might be asking for trouble.

157 **Rent a tandem bike** and participate in a charity bike ride. The tandem will equalize any differences in your physical ability. Raise money together, train together, and celebrate together. Research the AIDS rides (www.pallottateamworks.com) and the Pan-Massachusetts Challenge (www.pmc.org). If bicycling is not for you, do a charity walk together.

158 **Explore spirituality together.** Look for weekend retreats and evening lectures that challenge each of you to expand your thinking about life, death, or religion. Find a neutral topic that allows each of you to find yourself in the teachings, rather than something that requires a long-term commitment that only one of you may be willing to make. Meditation and yoga workshops make a lot of sense, because each of you can make your discoveries at your own level, with complete freedom.

159 Go to a theme park with your lover. Ride the Ferris wheel, holding hands. Find a scary ride that you both can handle.

160 Go on a compromise adventure. There is a place in your relationship where you and your partner are seemingly miles apart. Get creative. Propose three wacky compromises that will give each of you an acceptable new option. Explore the vast fertile ground that lives in the chasm between your two perspectives.

161 **Make a gift** for your lover. Make a customized CD of songs that remind you of him or her. Make brownies or a great meal. Make a piece of art. Too many people compulsively rush to the mall to find a token of love; something simple, made with your own two hands, may say much more.

162 **Create a scavenger hunt** in your bedroom. Write messages to your partner asking for what you want from them and what you want to give them in bed. Hide them in unusual places, like in the pockets of clothes seldom worn, at the bottom of sock drawers, and in shoes in the back of the closet.

163 **Spend at least an hour** every week researching the art of making love. Read books to one another about how to give and receive the highest levels of pleasure. If you already have a great sex life, go deeper and explore whole-body orgasms and tantric sex.

164

Take your partner on frequent nighttime walks. Explore the secretive quality of your neighborhood at night, as the energy of the day calms down and people go to sleep.

SELF

There is no more important relationship than the one you have with yourself. All other relationships are based on your self-assessment. As you practice self-acceptance and self-love, you will find that you are more able to accept others. As you deepen your relationship with yourself, many new relationships will open up for you. You'll not only have more patience, empathy, and compassion for other people, but you'll also become a magnet for people who are attracted to your strong core.

Your self-discovery is an ongoing and delicious adventure, yours in every moment. The adventures that follow will help you experience the adventure of self-love.

165 **Designate one day** a week as self-criticism free. Notice how frequently your self-critical machinery fires up. Each time you notice, grab the switch to shut it down. Do it every Tuesday, but change the name to support you on this challenging adventure; call that day of the week Tu-love-myself-day. Give yourself the freedom to be well and whole exactly how you are.

166 **Write down everything** for which you need to forgive yourself and then burn it, bury it, or float it down a river. Like everyone on the planet, you've made mistakes. Forgive yourself in a simple ritual today. You'll immediately be free to enjoy the glory of the present moment, once you let go of that weight in your life.

167 **Start a celebration** ritual each day to commemorate what you've accomplished.

Give yourself a five-minute gift at the end of every day. Close your eyes and appreciate what you did. Perform a celebratory dance to your favorite song. Read a segment of your favorite book. Do something that feels like a reward for a job well done. The adventure lies in acknowledging whatever you did for the day, even when you complete far less than you had intended.

168 Transform your relationship
with your "to do" list so that it no longer invalidates you. Most people use such a list irresponsibly and list far more than they could ever complete in a single day. Thus, the list is never completed and becomes evidence of your deficiency. It gnaws at you as if to suggest that if you were really worthy, you would finish it. Schedule less than you know you can do in a day. Move everything else to another day, delegate it, or let go of it. Change your "to do" list from something that makes you wrong into something that makes you right.

169 Trust your intuition. Spend a day without second-guessing. Follow your first instinct and, even though you'll always be able to question your decision after the fact, trust that you made the right choice. You already have more answers than you realize. Start listening and you'll get acquainted with a part of yourself you never really knew.

170 Listen to your body. Eat only when you are hungry. Sleep when you are tired. Share the feelings that come up. Listen to internal signals rather than masking them with caffeine or alcohol or suppressing them, even if that's what everyone else is doing.

171 Draw at least four self-portraits. Use only your left hand for two of them. Use a pencil or use multiple colors—there is no right way to do this. Display at least one of them on your refrigerator. What does this picture say about how you perceive yourself?

172 Try a self-indulgent adventure.

Schedule a block of time each week for a recurring gift of a series of classes followed by a great meal, during which you don't have to think about anyone other than yourself. Or plan a weekend morning when you can sleep late, simply for pure self-refreshment.

173 Have one TV-free night a week at home alone. Better still, turn off the cable for a month. Learn to love your own company. Cook something only you would appreciate. Put on your favorite music and dance through the house. Read the books you always wanted to read or go for a walk in the woods alone. You can be your own best friend and your greatest lover. Suspend the notion that you are loathsome. Embrace the possibility that you are the greatest companion you could ever have.

174 **Soak your feet.** Give yourself a weekly night of unconditional self-care. Groom every part of your body. Soak in a bubble bath. Turn your bathroom into your own personal spa and luxuriate. Learn to recharge and refresh within the confines of your own home. Hang a "do not disturb" sign and go deep inside your own personal evening retreat.

175 **Have a hobby budget.** Earmark 3 percent of your annual salary for something you absolutely love, with no agenda and no expectation other than to indulge yourself. Use that money to sign up for classes to learn French, plan a trip to France, or eat in a French restaurant once each quarter. Or use it to collect the one thing you always wanted. Enrich your relationship with yourself. Invest in a hobby right now.

176 **Make a contract** with yourself to set aside one hour every day for adventure.

Exercise. Walk around the neighborhood. Call friends. Do anything that would take you to an unfamiliar place. And make it a nonnegotiable agreement. If you can't make an hour for yourself every day, you're doing too much and you need to redesign the structure of your day. Nothing is more important than your health and well-being. If you end up sick, nothing in your life moves forward. So make your well-being your first priority.

177 Record your dreams. Keep a notebook by your nightstand and write them down when you first awake. Spend the day guided by your dreams. Listen to the messages delivered from your subconscious. Treat your dreams as telegrams from your soul and take them seriously. When they make no sense, share them with a friend and work to understand them.

178 Check out at least one self-development book on tape from the library every month. Let the author ride with you in your car on your way to work. He or she will take you on an adventure in their world. Listen to financial experts, success gurus, or teachings about God. Let your car be your temple and a place of great solo growth and development.

179 Set up a weekly outlet for your self-expression. Sing. Dance. Paint. Play guitar. Write. Make something out of wood or metal. If you feel like no one notices you or you don't exist, make art. Leave evidence of your creative genius behind. If none of these forms of expression speak to you, look through local adult-education catalogs and find something that does.

180 Take a meditation class. Learn to watch your thoughts course through your brain and acknowledge that they will always be there, beyond your control. Appreciate this fascinating mechanism and the automatic nature of your thoughts. Your

thoughts will forever defy your control. But you forever have an opportunity to manage your reactivity to those thoughts. Make self-development one of your hobbies, because when you can let your thoughts go without reacting to them, you will discover unprecedented freedom and forever-unexplored new ground.

181 **Do something** that is incredibly fun where you lose yourself and where your mind lets go. Find an activity that allows you to be free like a child. Don't use alcohol or drugs. Instead, actually do the one thing that would turn you on at this level.

182 **Do nothing.** Watch the trees blow. Notice the sea birds diving. Give yourself the gift of agenda-less time. And you'll be free.

183 **Leave your watch at home** for a day and let go of the hold time has on you.

184 **Give yourself** at least twelve "blow off" coupons. Use them when you really don't feel like going to events or going out. Stay home and deepen your relationship with yourself instead.

185 **Spend at least one weekend** a year without leaving your house. Make your home into your personal retreat center. Stop rushing all over town or running off to your country home. Fall in love with your current home instead.

186 **Do the things you want** to do even if you have to go alone. Many people use lack of companionship as an excuse that keeps them from local adventures. Give it up. Declare your independence.

Decide that you will not be stopped from attending an interesting lecture or class, even if you have to go alone.

187 **A good film** is one of the least expensive gifts you can give yourself. In fact, many libraries regularly show classics for free. See an inspirational film at least once a month. Or join a foreign film theatre and travel the world in movies from the comfort of a theatre seat. And go alone to deepen your adventure of self-respect. Should someone want to join you, that's fine. But don't let lack of company stop you from giving this adventurous gift to yourself.

188 **Think of something you want** today and actually ask for it. Go on a request adventure where you would usually hold your tongue. You might even discover that you get what you ask for! At the very least, you'll discover that you have the power and skill to ask for what you want.

189

Do something different. Somewhere in your life is something that has been frustrating. Something is not moving forward or someone isn't calling back. Don't call again and leave another message. Do something different. Go in a new direction and watch what happens.

A RELATIONSHIP FULL OF WONDER

Traffic was not moving at a downtown intersection.

A Wonder Bread truck had died at a red light on a hot day, snarling traffic, which was now honking for it to be more mature and move. I pulled alongside and there was the driver, reclining in his seat. The hood and the doors of the truck were wide open, as both the driver and the engine gasped for air. He was leaning back in his seat napping as he waited for help, oblivious to the jammed-up traffic all around him.

"At least you won't go hungry," I said.

"Got plenty of bread, " he replied, as he awoke to the world outside his immobile breadbox.

"Got any extra that's now going to go bad?" I asked.

Now, this inanimate man in an inanimate truck was coming to life and happy to play. He reached behind his seat into the back of the truck, ready to pass me a loaf like an All-American quarterback.

"No, no, I don't eat white bread, but thanks anyway. By the way, do you ever bring a jar of peanut butter and jelly to work and make a sandwich in the back of your truck after each delivery? You could last for days in there. Shouldn't every one of those trucks come with a jar of Skippy and a quart of milk, as standard equipment, just like the fire extinguisher?"

He laughed and said that he doesn't eat white bread either.

The light changed and I shifted into gear. We each waved good-bye, and as I drove off, he yelled, "Love your convertible!" as if he wanted to further nourish me from our traffic-light relationship adventure. In just thirty seconds we sure had a good time, just for the fun of it.

Even though I didn't eat it, Wonder Bread was the bread all my friends seemed to eat when I was a kid. That was before cable TV and back in the days when my mom was strange for buying Pepperidge Farm sprouted wheat. Thomas' hadn't even invented whole-wheat English muffins yet. I have to believe that a lot of people in that traffic jam also had childhood Wonder Bread memories. How come I was the only one being childlike with the Wonder Bread man?

a world of adventure within your body

A s you read this, you're gripping somewhere. Muscles are trying to hold on, keep control, or figure it out. Perhaps your eyebrows are tense, your jaw muscle is engaged, your breathing is shallow, you're clenching your butt, or your shoulders are slightly raised. You're working harder than necessary and you probably don't even notice. Whether conscious or unconscious, tension is blocking your ability to feel fully alive.

This chapter will launch you on a scavenger hunt of inquiry into that tension and an incredible adventure of exploration into your body. You'll find new paths to letting go and you'll enhance your health and well-being at the same time. Body consciousness gives you the power to intervene and to make changes in your daily habits so that you can increase your longevity. And the real beauty of body adventures is that they are completely customized and personal. You get to be the ultimate judge of what does and doesn't work for your particular body. This is an ongoing adventure that you get to enjoy for the rest of your life.

Engage this adventure from exactly where you are right now, regardless of your opinion of your body. As with every adventure in this book, your history will not thwart your adventures. The only prerequisite is that you are alive. Our bodies are constantly cycling, changing, and evolving in a lifelong flow. With childlike fascination, let's see how much we can discover. I hope to open your eyes to this rich and often unexplored world.

Start with your definition of your body. Do you see yourself as short, lanky, of medium or athletic build, stout, or lean? Most people reduce their bodies to a brief description. But this rich universe of processes, systems, and magical automatic functions cannot be reduced to one word. Moreover, that one word is often what we perceive to be our greatest shortcoming. Do you describe yourself as "average"? There is nothing average about any body. Herein lies the rich adventure. You should define your body with a whole chapter and not just a few words. Our body is the only thing we have for our entire life. We think we know it but we have only just begun to understand.

Much of the adventure available to you in body exploration involves stripping away preconceived notions about who you are as defined by your body. You are not that too much/too little/just perfect weight anymore than you are your car or your career. Let go of your attachment to the notion that your body is who you are. Let go of your picture of how you should look. Instead, celebrate your spirit, regardless of your features, size, or weight. You'll find the freedom to discover the true depth of your beauty.

In yoga class one Friday, we were leaning back over the bases of chairs to open our upper chests in preparation for back bends. My head hung toward the middle of the room. Across the class, I could see seven of my peers also hanging upside down. They looked so peaceful, stretching their hearts and hanging inverted. They looked as though they were flying in their dreams, arms outstretched, rolling and gliding among the clouds. In moments like these, I am in awe of what we can discover in our own bodies. Yoga had supported a group of very busy and often serious folks to find angelic beauty, on an adventure of body discovery that anyone can share.

BREATHE

Your breath is the gateway to discovery in your body. Breath gives you access to new worlds, and all you need to do is bring your attention to it. You don't need to be a yogi or learn to meditate to use your breath for adventurous self-discovery (although yoga and meditation are well worth exploring). Even at a traffic light or waiting for your toast to pop, you can discover power and capacities you never realized you had. Learn to move your breath with skill, just as you would move any other part of your body. Let breathing become an adventure, rather than a routine.

190 **Place one hand on your belly** and the other on your chest. Keeping the hand on your belly still, breathe just through your chest. Then switch, and just breathe through your belly. Next, try breathing like an ocean wave, inhaling first from your belly and then from your chest, then exhaling from your chest and then your belly. Discover how much more air you can move with this technique.

191

Once you master breathing like a wave, find a third tier by pulling your breath even higher into the very top portion of your lungs, just beneath your collarbones. Breathe in through your belly, chest, collarbones, then out through your collarbones, chest, and belly. Let your breath wash through your entire upper body and celebrate; even though you have been breathing all your life, you've just found new breathing capacity! Practice while you wait. Every checkout line is an invitation to play with your breath. A trip to the DMV is an opportunity for an extended breath safari.

192

Imagine a balloon inside your head that you can expand and contract as you inhale and exhale. With each breath, feel your brain expand fully against your skull as you inflate your lungs, and then relax as you exhale. Try reversing the sequence; contract the balloon while you inhale and let it expand on the exhalation. Explore your power to heal headaches. Learn to wash your brain with vitality.

193 **Use your breath** for an adventure of self-esteem. When you are feeling threatened, intimidated, or small, keep slowly and deliberately exhaling as you imagine that you can fill the room with your own invisible smoke. Direct your breath around the room by moving your head slowly from side to side as you blow through your mouth. Imagine that your energy fills the space so completely and so powerfully that you will have no trouble asking for what you need, making a speech, or saying what's on your mind.

194 **Discover new ways** to initiate your breath. Instead of inhaling as you normally would, pull your stomach muscles and diaphragm downward, so that your breath effortlessly flows inward like a waterfall.

195 **Massage your back** on a breathing adventure. Expand your lower back as you

inhale, pushing it deep into your office chair to relax the chronic tension you hold there. Try the same thing with your upper back, too.

196 **You know your face** in the mirror; now get to know it from the inside out. Close your eyes and use your exhalation to soften all your facial muscles so that your face feels as though it is just hanging on the front of your head. You'll melt away tension you didn't even know was there.

197 **Launch an exhalation** exploration. Exhale your way to work. As you walk to your office, inhale five paces, and then exhale ten paces. Purge all the stale air you hold in your lungs.

198 **As you wait** for someone to answer, let the sound of the ringing phone in your ear send you on an adventure into your shoulders. With every ring, exhale fully to melt the tension in the shoulder beneath the handset. Instead of listening to that sound solely with anticipation of the other person answering, use these precious moments to go deeper into your shoulder as you relax it to a new level. Ideally, you'd have a headset telephone, and use this time to find new levels of relaxation in both shoulders.

199 Cover your dashboard clock

with a stick-on note that says "time to breathe," and see if you can make your next trip through traffic into a breathing adventure. While driving to appointments, I often find myself compulsively turning my head to the right to check my dashboard clock and see if I'll make it on time. Only when I realized that no amount of clock checking would alter my arrival time did I discover that I could use this impulse to my advantage. Now, each time I get the urge, I keep my eyes on the road and take a deep breath instead.

200 **Use your exhalation** as an important piece of adventure gear, just like Indiana Jones's whip. When you notice that you are afraid, see how long you can exhale. Blow out every last bit of breath and let your fear go with it. Try this on the elevator as you ascend to an uncomfortable business meeting. You'll arrive at your floor ready for anything. Fear is part of any good adventure. Don't deny it. Use your breath to discover an exciting new way to move through it.

201 **Take a deep breath** and see if one side of your chest feels dominant. Bring your focus to the other lung and try to equalize your breath. Play with this new consciousness the next time you're working out and need additional capacity.

202 **Wash your eyeballs with vitality.** Close your tired eyes and bring your inhalation up the left side of each eye and descend your exhalation on the right. Reverse the flow; up the right, down the left. Let fresh oxygen envelop and nourish each eye.

203 **Discover your tail.** Bring your focus to your coccyx. Breathe through it by contracting the base of your spine on the inhalation and relaxing it on exhalation. This is a useful breath to practice while sitting at your desk or while driving.

FEET AND HANDS

Your feet take millions of steps for you but you probably only stop to notice them when they hurt. A world of micro movements goes on just beneath the tongue of your sneakers. With new consciousness, you'll discover that your funny feet are actually fun. Likewise, your hands play the violin, carry wood, type all day on the computer, and allow you to experience the soft fur on the underbelly of your cat. How could we take such magic for granted? Tune into the little adventure of your extremities, with every step on your way to work and with every button you push on the keypad of your phone.

204 **Imagine** that the tips of your toes can inhale. Breathe deeply and draw air up through your shoes, through your legs, and up to your lungs. Find the connection between your upper and lower bodies with your breath. Do this while performing mundane tasks to liven up the activity.

205 **Bring your wrists** out in front of your chest and shake your hands vigorously for a thirty-second energy adventure. Relax them completely and let your fingers and wrists hang limp as you shake. You'll start to feel energy between your thumbs and pinky fingers. Use this technique the next time your hands get cold.

206 Wake up your fingers. Move each one to its full range and appreciate your dexterity. Maintain a natural gap between each finger and extend them outward simultaneously, as though to make them longer. Exhale and feel energy emanate from your fingertips.

207 Gather a ball of energy. While extending you fingers outward, bring your hands together, as if you were going to clap, but move them as slowly as you can. Feel the energy gather between your hands. Stop when you feel resistance. You should feel a ball of energy gather between your hands. Play with your new energy discovery. It may feel like a big beach ball or smaller, perhaps tennis-ball size. Roll each hand from 3 and 9 o'clock to 6 and 12, both clockwise and counterclockwise, as though you were holding a delicate sphere. Inhale deeply and press both hands to your belly to draw the energy sphere into your center for a dose of natural stimulant.

208 **Practice** using your nondominant hand. If you are right handed, practice brushing your teeth with your left hand. Scoop dinner out of the pot with your left hand. Eat with your left hand. Train yourself to be more ambidextrous. See if this practice will bring you new creativity and a more balanced perspective of your life.

209 **Your hands mirror your heart.** Walk normally with your arms at your side, but face your palms forward. Sit in meetings with your hands at your sides, palms forward. You'll open your chest and your heart so that more love can flow in and out.

210 **Your feet determine** how you connect to the rest of the world. As you stand, make sure that you have a 50/50 weight distribution on your feet, so that you are completely grounded. Rock left and right, fore and aft, to find a new center.

211 **Nest your fingers** between each of your toes. Acknowledge all ten of them. When did you last communicate with each one individually? Weave your other hand through them from the other side of your foot. Isolate each one of them. Meet the individual muscles of each toe.

212 **Close your eyes** and have someone gently touch the tip of one of your toes. See if you can call out which toe it was. Learning to attune yourself to subtle sensations can make you more available for the hidden adventures of everyday life.

213 **Put two tennis balls** under your desk and roll your bare feet on top of them. Rest your feet on the balls while you are on the phone to wake up the muscles in your feet. Spiny massage balls work even better.

214 **Notice your toes** on your next walk to the office. Are they gripping your shoes? Paddling down the sidewalk? Fluttering in the breeze? Can you relax them?

215 **Change your gait.** Caress a cushion of energy just above the sidewalk as you walk. Lift your feet just enough so that they're gliding along the ground. Have you been wasting energy lifting your feet higher than necessary with every step?

216 **Walk on your heels.** You've walked from the train or your car to your office hundreds of times before. Make your next trip an adventure. Walk on the balls of your feet, then the heels. Try just the outsides and then just the insides of your shoes. Then see if you can use all four of these portions of your feet with every step. Roll your entire foot over the sidewalk like a steamroller. Pretend that your name is engraved in a

rubber stamp on the bottoms of your soles. Leave a perfect imprint of every letter with every step. Next, walk lightly, like a deer, barely touching the earth. Leave the shallowest footprints on the concrete. Pretend you are walking on fragile ice and you don't want to break through.

217 The next time your boss calls you into his office, play an adventurous game that will make you invincible. Imagine the roots of a powerful tree flowing out of each toe every time your foot contacts the ground. As you transfer weight onto your foot, the roots fire outward, rip through the concrete, and dive into the ground. As you step off that foot, the roots retract back into your feet and the concrete magically seals back up again. Make "swamp thing" sound effects, as your roots fire and then rip out of the ground with every step.

218 **Walk with your heart,** not your feet. On your next trip to meet someone you like, bring all the focus to your chest, See if your feet glide with you as your heart guides you down the street. Be an angel—flow to your destination, effortlessly.

219 **Change your shoes** midday. See if your day changes.

220 **Try a session** with a foot reflexologist. Call a spa. Look in the Yellow Pages, or search the Web to find one. They're as common in Asia as dry cleaners are in America. Discover why.

SENSES

You are gifted with tremendous sensitivity. How much do you use? Stretch the boundaries of what you sense, like an adventurer looking for treasure. Bring more attention to your senses and see if the range is just a bit broader than you have assumed for all of your life. Remember your first kiss, when time stood still in a divine moment as two sets of lips connected? In this section, you'll have an opportunity to bring first-kiss sensitivity to your entire body and all its functions. Each of your senses represents a different part of the body's playground, big enough for a lifetime of adventurous exploration and entertainment.

Touch

221 **Appreciate every inch** of your body as a conduit for sensuality and pleasure. You carry on your skin an entire world of nerve endings that you have never met. Wake them up today. Experiment with a soft body brush. Apply some massage oil and rub the brush all over your hand and arm (or preferably, have your lover do so for you). Swirl the bristles in a circular motion, particularly in between your fingers. As the brush gently passes over your skin, feel the expansive sensitivity on your arms, the backs of your hands, and your wrists. Swirl the brush up the inside of your elbows. Discover your extreme touch sensitivity without even getting close to your obvious pleasure centers.

222 A simple greeting is an opportunity to explore your ability to touch. The next time you shake hands with someone, really feel their hand in yours. In that single second as two hands come together, notice the texture, temperature, and firmness of the hand that meshes with yours. Don't just shake hands on auto-pilot. Feel the hand of another human being. Connect with them at that magical moment, through touch.

223 A kiss on the cheek also provides a touch adventure. Don't just go through the motions on automatic. Actually participate. Don't slow it down so much that you are inappropriate or suggestive. Simply take an extra half-second and feel the connection with another human being through your lips.

224 **Somewhere between hugging** with your butt sticking out to avoid any body contact and hugging your lover lies a hugging adventure. Find a way to connect more acreage of your body in every hug, without making it suggestive or inappropriate, so that you actually feel the person you choose to hug.

SMELL

225 **Visit a florist** to see which scents evoke powerful memories from your past. Energize your home with a bouquet that reminds you of something wonderful.

226 **Go fragrance free** and get to know the natural smell of your partner.

227 **Surprise your lover** with an adventurous new perfume or cologne and see if a new scent alters the quality of your date.

228 **Experiment** with essential oils; few things on Earth hold so much power in just a few drops. Put a drop of lavender on your pillow before you go to sleep if you are feeling stressed and see if you wake up feeling refreshed. A few drops of eucalyptus can turn your bathtub into a relaxing decongestant. Get a book on aromatherapy and see if it's an art worth further exploration.

229 **Take a deep breath** just outside your door. What is the smell of the season?

If you live downwind from a factory, drive out of town to the woods and take your nose for a walk.

TASTE

230 **Take your taste buds** on an adventure. Instead of the same old supermarket, visit a different one and sample an assortment of unfamiliar foods. Try a health-food supermarket, a Chinese market, or an Indian one.

231 **Take a trip** to a foreign land by exploring the herbal tea aisle of your supermarket. What if such a simple drink could alter your mood or enhance your memory? Try Kava Kava and Ginkgo to see for yourself.

232 **Discover the spice** that fits you like a glove. Once I found the strong cinnamon and chicory flavor of Celestial Seasonings Bengal Spice tea, I felt as if I had met an old friend. Everyone should search for their favorite taste with the same passion they would apply to the search for the right job or lover.

233 **Try a pomegranate,** persimmon, or Anjou pear. The produce department of a good supermarket sells at least one hundred fruit and vegetable adventures. Sample a tangelo, Mineola, and blood orange. Bring home your first Macoun, Cameo, Gala, or Winesap apple. Anticipate the special moment when first you bite into what could be the perfect palate-pleasing blend of tart and sweet.

234 **Expand the world** of what you eat. Taste something unfamiliar on every visit to the market. Ask the fish man what's particularly fresh. Try a new cut of meat. Sample a new kind of cookie.

235 **Step outside** the boring world of peanuts; sample different nuts. Get to know filberts and hazelnuts, pumpkin seeds and sunflower seeds, in and out of their shells. Instead of peanut butter, try macadamia-nut and pistachio-nut butter.

236 **Explore the world** of pure dairy products. Buy organic milk and butter. See if you can taste the difference in products that are pesticide free. Better still, visit a local farm for your milk and eggs. Watch the cows being milked and ask to taste milk processed that same day.

237 **Journey into vegetable bliss.** Taste a plantain. Buy shallots instead of onions. Taste a new kind of lettuce. Sample some watercress and frisee. Learn the difference between kale and escarole. Go beyond green beans and corn. Try organic radishes and arugula.

238 Find the places in your mouth that actually do the tasting. Do you taste on only one part of your tongue? Does the rest of your mouth send cues about the taste of your food? Tune into the source of taste. Notice the subtle ways you experience taste.

239 Take an international food vacation. You don't need to travel overseas to enjoy the experience of your country of choice. Buy lunch from the Japanese market. Get fresh pasta at an Italian market. Purchase at least one product with foreign-language directions. Ask the store owner to translate the instructions. Then try to make it at home. Try Hungarian cooking. Check out cookbooks from the library and experiment with food from around the globe.

240 Spend a week eating kale, spinach, or a similar leafy green as a generous side dish every night and see if you notice any difference in how you feel.

241 **Go to food specialty shops** and tell them you are on an international adventure, looking to sample the finest foods of their country. Visit the German butcher or Thai grocery and ask what they would suggest for dinner. The proprietor will likely be delighted to share their passion and to give you all the instructions you need so you can cook with regional flare. They might even invite you to dinner at their house!

242 **Buy honey** from a local beekeeper. Ask to meet the bees. Buy maple syrup from local trees and help collect it. Pure foods direct from their source will deepen your relationship with taste.

243 **Go on a $20 taste bud** adventure. Tell a gourmet shop owner you want to learn about their world. Put the $20 on the counter and ask to taste an assortment of cheeses, chocolates, coffees, or meats from around the world.

244 **Spend $10 in the spice aisle** at the supermarket. Get to know the flavor of coriander seeds, cumin, and cardamom.

245 **Get to know the difference** between generic and super premium ice cream. Try something other than vanilla, chocolate, or strawberry—like ginger, red bean, or green tea ice cream (available at many Japanese restaurants and markets).

246 **At the French bakery,** sample the various varieties of baguettes. They look similar but there are subtle differences in texture, flour, cooking method, and size. Instead of packaged bread, buy fresh bread each day from the bakery.

247 **Visit the wine store** and sample wines from different countries. Compare

$10 bottles from Australia and South America. Learn the difference between wine from Napa and Sonoma in California or Bordeaux and Burgundy in France. There may also be a beer hiding in the cooler that tastes much better than your regular brand. Have some fun searching for it. Try at least six new brands.

248 Try an unusual juice drink. If you don't drink alcohol, you can have just as much fun trying black currant, boysenberry, and ginger echinacea juice. You don't even have to go to the islands.

249 Visit a new restaurant at least once each month. Look for a Tibetan or Ethiopian restaurant. Try sushi, Korean barbecue, Vietnamese, and Thai. Try a natural-food restaurant and see if you feel any different after eating healthy food. Try as many different cuisines as your budget allows. Travel the world with your tongue.

250 **Let the subtle flavor** of water train your tastebuds. Close your eyes and try two different bottled waters. Learn to appreciate the varied taste in this "tasteless" liquid and search for the water you love best.

HEAR

251 **Celebrate your power** to hear. Put on your favorite music, close your eyes, and really listen. Don't just leave music on in the background; bring it to the foreground of your life. Look for the subtle variations and instruments in the music. Listen to the lyrics. Enjoy mindfully listening to the music.

252 **Bring your favorite CD** to a high-end stereo store and ask to sample a new system. Sit in a listening room and savor the acoustic adventure.

253 **Treat your ears** to an international journey. Head to the library and choose a dozen varied world music CDs you can sample at home.

254 **Attend an intimate concert** in a small coffeehouse or club. Enjoy a new sensory experience.

255 **Let nature train your ears** to tune into the subtleties of sound. Sit by a river or an ocean with your eyes closed and focus exclusively on the sound. In a rainstorm, lie on the floor with your eyes closed and the windows open. These soothing natural sounds will transport you on a blissful auditory adventure.

256 **Walk in the woods** and tune into the sounds of your feet on the dry leaves on the trail. Try this in the rain and listen to the reflective sound of fresh raindrops hitting upward-cupped leaves. Try this in the winter once the leaves have flattened out and notice the subtle sound change.

257 **Get to know the difference** between the call of the cat bird and screech of the red-tailed hawk. Appreciate your ability to identify the birds around your house, exclusively with your ears.

TRUST YOUR INSTINCTS

258 **Spend an entire day** listening to your internal guidance system. When you have a feeling that something is right or wrong, act on it. Don't do anything reckless, irresponsible, or illegal. Just resist the temptation to conduct your normal exhaustive analysis as you attempt to find the right answer. Embrace your first impulse instead.

259 **Your instincts** also tell you how other people feel about you. Try inquiring. If you sense someone likes or dislikes you, mention it and engage the world of intuition that's been with you all along.

260 **Decline everything** that doesn't feel right. Go toward whatever you sense will work out, even if it's unproven. This adventure is no less exciting than climbing a mountain. Listen. Your body will guide you.

MOVEMENT

Most of our movements are unconscious, even though life is always moving. Many adults seem to confine their movement to walking and an occasional workout, often in front of a TV in a health club. Adulthood fuses otherwise independent pieces of our bodies as we settle into a limited range of motion. Adventure lives on the fringes of that range. Reach just a bit outside of what you know your body can do and explore what's possible with a sense of wonder. Go on an adventure to reclaim the freedom of movement you had as a child. Learn what's possible for your unique body.

261 **Choose a sport** you love and find other people who like to play it. Start an after-work volleyball league. Organize intramural soccer. Sign up for the racquetball ladder at your health club. Join an ultimate Frisbee team. Rent a ski house with friends. Find a way to put movement back into your life on a regular basis and rediscover what your body can do.

262 **Try at least one** new sport every year. Rather than lament your lack of proficiency, celebrate your body's ability to learn and to balance, regardless of your skill level. Be a beginner, free of expectation of mastery, and enjoy the new adventure.

263 **Run up a streambed,** jumping from rock to rock. Reconnect with your sense of balance and agility. Risk getting wet feet.

264 **Compete.** Try at least one local race. Look in the local free sports newspaper for schedules. Consider triathlons, marathons, 10K runs, swimming competitions, road and mountain bike races, adventure-team races, rock-climbing competitions, Nastar ski races, and Rollerblade races. Visit a shop in your area that sells the best equipment for your sport. They can help you schedule your training and direct you to local competitions. Competition will push you to the edge of your comfort zone, to a place you might not have visited before.

265 **Commit to a season of racing** and make training a regular part of your weekly schedule. Do so with a friend and make your training a social event. Your performance relative to others is irrelevant. Your discovery of your own potential is more important. Don't be ashamed to start in the beginner class. You'll still challenge your perceptions about your body. Are your limits largely in your mind?

266 **Understand the fuels** that make your body operate at its peak. Learn your body's specific nutritional needs. What's the right mix of protein and carbohydrates for your unique body? This inquiry will reward you with increased athletic performance, health, and vitality.

267 **Train with a heart monitor.** You can buy them at bike and running shops or outdoor store like EMS or REI. Learn your resting and target heart rates. The monitor will help you deepen your relationship with your circulatory system as you explore parts of your body you have taken for granted.

268 **Don't just run;** tune in to your full stride. Notice where your feet contact the ground and how you move your arms. Don't just ride your bike; learn to use new muscles as you pull up on the pedals. Don't just swim; focus on the quality of the connection between your strokes. Consciousness will help you find new fluidity in your movements.

269 **Make yoga a part of your life** and you'll facilitate a lifelong adventure of movement, which I've found more adventurous than learning to fly an airplane. You don't need to amass any more expensive adventure gear or buy a new attachment for your roof rack. Inside your body, you already have all the right equipment, regardless of your skill level. Explore the world of yoga classes right in your own town. Sample the various styles; you'll learn something new from each teacher and discipline. Hatha yoga tends to be extremely gentle and relaxing. Bikram's yoga is studied in a heated studio. Iyengar yoga is a very technical and sometimes extremely regimented style of yoga, which incorporates numerous props to facilitate entry into the various postures.

270 **Commit to two** yoga classes each week. Have a friend photograph you in a few poses when you start. Compare those photos to pictures taken a year later and see how much flexibility you've discovered.

271 **Make dance a regular practice.** Taking classes will keep you probing into what's possible for your body. Don't let either your training or, alternatively, your lack of experience stop you; there is a class for every dancer. Try dancekinetics, NIA, trance dance, or any other free form dance class. These classes emphasize complete acceptance of every kind of movement. Surrender to the music in class and you will experience complete dancing freedom. Look in your area for a wellness center. They should know who offers such classes.

272 **Dance around the world** by sampling assorted ethnic dance classes. Look in the Yellow Pages under "Dance" and try African, Haitian, Cuban, or South American dance classes. Try jazz, tap, ballroom, and salsa, or line dance, square dance, or anything else that interests you.

273 **Buy a rubber flex ball** designed for fitness and balance. Lie on this beach ball on your stomach, back, and sides twice each day. Daily life often closes people down and effectively shuts out new discoveries. The ball will open your body back up again and you'll certainly find new flexibility and balance. When you roll out of bed in the morning, lie on the ball and wake up the adventurous liquidity of all your joints.

274 **Massage a partner** at the same time. Face each other on all fours. Gently press the crowns of your heads together. Slowly shake your head as though you were gesturing "no" while maintaining contact. Then try gesturing "yes" and let different portions of your heads make contact. While still facing one another on all fours, now move your left ear alongside your partner's left ear and press the top of your head into the muscles on top of your partner's shoulder. Have your partner do the same. Gently press forward to massage your partner's shoulder muscles. Switch sides and press into the other shoulder. You'll each enjoy a simultaneous massage.

DEEPER EXPLORATION

We traditionally think that adventure lives outside someplace...in the jungle, on a mountaintop, certainly outside our front door. But there is an adventure waiting for you inside your body, which is a classroom for the unlimited possibilities of life. Look deep inside, with the same fascination you would otherwise reserve for deplaning in a foreign land. Challenge the hopelessness you hold about your body, given your physical age or stereotypes.

We tend to notice the physical abilities that we have lost as we age, not what we acquire. We have cultural notions like "You're not a teenager anymore," as if to suggest that we have to stop our physical exploration and wait for our death behind a desk. I'm not suggesting that a fifty-year-old executive jump into a college rugby match. But I am suggesting that there are pieces of your body you haven't yet met, regardless of your age. Look inward. Challenge what you think you know about how your body works.

275 **Stare into your own eyes** in the bathroom mirror for at least thirty seconds. Notice the unique, multicolored shape in the center of your eye. Notice how your irises are not symmetrical and how each one has a magical pattern, like the most beautiful crystal on earth. Inhale deeply as you distinguish this incredible artwork, which is forever a part of you.

276 **Spend an entire day** looking at this artwork in the eyes of the people you meet. Look for the natural gems in their eyes and know that in so doing, you are displaying yours with pride and majesty. Everyone you meet sees you through this filter.

277 **Lie flat on your back** on the floor, like a corpse. Make sure your arms and legs make no contact with anything other than the floor. Gently close your eyes and breathe deeply while you scan your body for tension. Start at the tips of your toes and move upward, searching and releasing anything that's tight. Surrender to the floor. Relax your legs, your back, your tongue, and your eyebrows. Courageously vaporize all the tension operating in the background, just out of your view. After five minutes, you'll get up feeling energized and then you can explore what it's like to meet the rest of your workday with a relaxed attitude.

278

Learn to manipulate the secret control panel that dissolves tension in your head. Place the three middle fingertips of each hand about one inch above and parallel to your eyebrows. Press your fingers into the small trough that runs across your forehead from one temple to the other. Move your fingers laterally very slowly, stopping anywhere there is increased sensitivity. Press into the sensitive areas with your fingertips in a gentle circular motion. Move your fingers all around your forehead and temples in search of more tender spots. Find all the switches—you may find you've discovered a new way to get rid of a headache.

279

Recharge your batteries. Rub your hands together vigorously until your hands get very warm. Exhale deeply as you rub. Then place your warm hands over your eyes and inhale all the energy generated by your wonderful hands. Even if you think your hands are unattractive, they do work at your command and create your art with grace, on both the computer and piano keyboard, or wherever else you make art in your life. As you learn to respect your hands as a gift regardless of your opinion of their appearance, you can learn to accept the energized magic in all your body parts regardless of how you think they look.

280 **Spend five minutes** looking at yourself naked in a full-length mirror. Pretend you are an animal that makes no effort to hide its skin. You are as unique and beautiful as any cat, bird, or bug on the planet. Don't shy away from the mirror because you don't like some part of your body. Then go do your dishes naked. Clean the house and pay your bills naked. Come back to the mirror and spend five more minutes looking to see if your reactions are any different.

281 **Have your lover take a photo** of your naked body once each month for a year (or use the self-timer on your camera). Review all twelve pictures at year-end and notice the body you had for the year. Compare the pictures to the body that you expected to have. This exercise will help you on a journey of unconditional acceptance.

282 **Take a luxurious bath** at least once each week. Be a creature of nature, comfortable in your skin. Float in the warm water, revealed, without a layer of Mr. Bubble concealing your body. Get in the bath without an agenda; just float. Showers are too functional. Use your bathtub as a place to just be.

283 **Sleep naked.** If you traditionally sleep in pajamas or a nightgown, interrupt your fully clothed twenty-four-hour routine. Let your nights be a time to return to your elemental nakedness.

284 Find your heart. Lie on your back on your bed and slide over the side so that your shoulder blades just catch the edge of the bed. Slowly lower your head and arms over the side. Open your upper back and let your heart come forward in a gentle backbend. Breathe through your chest to open up all the protective layers surrounding your heart. Your heart may have taken a beating at some point in your life so you understandably retracted it into your chest. Let your heart come forward to take a more dominant role in your life once again. You can try the same stretch by leaning back so that the top of a chair catches you across your shoulder blades.

285 Put yourself in the hands of your hairstylist. Ask them to make you look your best. Let them alter your hairstyle so that it best suits your body.

286 **Choose the best-dressed** salesperson at your favorite clothing store and ask them to choose an outfit that perfectly fits your body type. Try it on, take a Polaroid picture, and put it on your refrigerator with your favorite magnet. See if you like your new image as it greets you every morning for breakfast. If so, go back and buy it.

287 **Go to a hat store** and ask the sales help to choose the hat that they feel best complements your body. Wear a beret or a fedora. Be a cowboy. Add some style to the top of your head, just for the fun of it.

288 **Wear adventurous jewelry.** Make a bold statement with the jewelry you choose. All men should wear a necklace at least once in their life. For women, try a toe ring or a temporary henna tattoo that covers your entire hand.

289 **Your underwear drawer** is a display of your adventurous spirit. Phase out your all white underthings. Buy at least five pairs of wild underwear, including at least one animal print.

290 **Take time out** for a healing adventure. Sit still for sixty seconds every morning and reflect on your ailments. Breathe deeply and bring your focus to your ulcer, headache, or backache. Don't just take a pill and run. Explore what your body can do. Spend just a minute being with your discomfort before you obliterate the pain with drugs.

291 **Challenge your relationship** with the physical age of your body. Don't shy away from your birthday celebration because you don't want to bring attention to aging. Instead, throw a party to celebrate the wisdom and experience that you have gained from another year on the planet. Invite your friends to share what they have learned since last year. Support one another by acknowledging the deep self-knowledge that comes with age.

CONSCIOUS SLEEPING

292 **Buy new sheets.** Get a mattress that supports you. Make your bed a shrine for your rest, healing, and recovery. Whether encased in flannel, satin, or plain cotton, make sure your bed is a special and comfortable place well worth climbing into. Don't take your bed for granted anymore. Create a custom magic carpet to take you on a deep journey of sleep.

293 **Experiment** with the amount you sleep. Research what your body needs and alter your habits accordingly. Try going to bed early at least one night a week and see how you feel. Do you need a constant amount of sleep? If you sleep eight hours, are you more tired than if you sleep for seven?

294 **Each night** before you fall asleep, lie on your back and gently run your hands down your face, from your forehead to your neck. Relax all the muscles in your face. Surrender all the masks you have worn throughout your day and fall asleep with a new expression of peace.

295 **Start on your back** before you fall asleep, even if you will ultimately move to another position. Keep your limbs from contacting any walls, partners, pets, or footboards. Don't cross your legs; and leave your arms outstretched. Float on the mattress, simultaneously completely free and supported. This is one place in your day where you are sure to find peace.

296 **Experiment** with your hand position as you sleep. Sleep with your palms down if you give too much and you feel depleted. Turn your hands up as you drift off to sleep as an expression of

your openness, and maybe you'll invite more opportunity and relationships into your life. Notice any color changes behind your closed eyes as you experiment with the various left-and-right, up-and-down hand combinations.

297 **Dreams** offer a chance to explore your subconscious. Attempt to cause your dreams to be memorable tonight. In Richard Bach's *Bridge across Forever*, the main characters go to sleep together intending to meet in their dreams. Try to meet someone you love in your dreams tonight.

298 **Turn the sheets** around on your bed. Sleep with your head at the opposite side. Switch places with your spouse. Sleep on the other side of the bed. Switch beds. Sleep in a different room. I find that such changes cause me to dream more vividly. Keep a journal next to your bed and write down your dreams as soon as you wake up. Create your personal book of adventures by capturing your dreams.

THE ADVENTURE OF DANCE

I'm holding Leslie Roberts close, locked in an adolescent slow dance. Shuffle right foot, shuffle left, all while in a slow clockwise, then counterclockwise, circle. We are not dancing, as much as hugging in a circular stumble. As the music ends, the lights dim and we lock in a long, closed-mouth kiss. Summer camp. I was twelve.

I never did learn to dance. Somehow, all I ended up knowing how to do was a stiff and lifeless shuffle, hopelessly stuck in 1973, at Camp Laurel in Readfield, Maine. For most of my adult life, I avoided dancing. I didn't dance.

Twenty-five years after my last summer-camp social, I went to my first dance class, all in the name of adventure. I remember an anxious, dry-mouthed feeling driving to class, scared I'd be too clumsy to follow. My fear nearly paralyzed me.

I arrived at an old barn for an evening of free-form dance, where every move is the right move. We started with yoga stretches, which were easy for me. And then the live drums got inside me and I had to move.

I poured like honey through thick connected movements, marched like a soldier, and kicked like a martial artist, leapt and let go. The evening was an orchestrated yet free-form rush of skipping, twisting, flying, and finally melting into my body until I released all the tension I had stored up all those years. Around and around, until my joints could flow, the muscles and the cells releasing with each spin. Finally, I was dancing.

Forty years of moving through my life; skiing, windsurfing, skating, climbing, biking...and here was an entirely new body adventure full of infinite movement. I actually thought I knew how to move before dance taught me that I just scratched the surface. Dance is so self-contained. Inside my body lives all the sporting equipment required. After a lifetime amassing mountains of assorted gear, I finally found a moving adventure for which I already had all the right equipment.

The next day, my face in the mirror looked lighter, softened by my dance. Happiness also seemed more accessible. I danced with hip gyrations as I moved from toaster to refrigerator. I swirled my shoulders as I cut the muffins. I rhythmically rolled my head as I did dishes. I've fed my cats twice a day for years, but never had I ratcheted my hips downward to the cat-food beat as I compressed to find their food on the lowest refrigerator shelf. Each step was like a novel toy. I wondered how my organs dance. What is the rhythm of digestion as my food goes on its long journey?

A month later, I registered for a series of jazz classes. I remember the warm-up in the first class. We slowly raised our arms out to the side and up over our heads, feeling energy move through our arms and imagining that our fingernails were so long that we could rub them along the walls and past the joint where the walls meet the ceiling. I saw a blissful look on the instructor's face as she did this. She wasn't just smiling for an imaginary audience. She was feeling something deep and her face was the picture of pure joy.

In that same class a year later, I saw that same look on my face in the mirror. I not only learned to dance but also to move blocked energy through my body and to connect with muscles I didn't know I could control. When I started these classes, I'd try to move just my neck when we did isolation exercises and my shoulders would move as well. Adulthood had fused independent pieces of my body. On my adventure of making my pieces independent again, I learned what's possible with my body, the one and only possession that will be with me for my entire life.

career
adventures

That thing that you do everyday, which you have labeled "your job"—familiar, static, recurring, and constant in your life—is actually an extremely fertile ground for adventure. In fact, the minute you think of your daily life as a job or a career or some sort of destination, you lose the true richness and joy available to you in all the present moments between nine and five. Life at the workplace is no different than life while you are on vacation, once you start to see that your life is not compartmentalized or limited to joy and adventure only during certain times of the year. Your workplace is one of your greatest adventures waiting to happen.

Embark on an adventure that takes you to an unrecognizable place where you absolutely love what you do in your workday. It is possible to love your work so much that you can't believe you get paid for what you do. This may require a transition from your current job, and it may take years, but you can start just where you are and little by little, you can make even your existing workplace more adventurous, a place where you look forward to going.

DECORATE

The place to start is with your physical space. Make your office or cubicle into your own personal cave. You'll probably spend more time in your office than you will in the living room of your house. Put time into decorating it so that you are enveloped in an atmosphere that supports you to be your adventurous best. Don't just move around the furniture. Instead, go for broke and make your office into a place you love to visit so much that you might even want to spend fifty hours a week there.

Your workspace should be a nurturing expression of who you are. It should be decorated so that your physical surroundings call you to be your authentic self. It has to provide you with all the tools to launch your adventure. Equip it for the journey that lies ahead. Whether you work on a fishing boat, drive a cab, spend your day in a ticket booth or in a corner suite, there is a way for you to personalize your workspace to optimize your adventurous career.

299 **Surround yourself** with pictures of loved ones. Customize your screen saver and mouse pad with artwork depicting your favorite things. Depict the places in your life where time stands still and where you are blissfully at peace, or the places where you feel most excited and full of energy. Your courageous voyage toward workplace bliss can only be called an adventure. These totems will support you on your journey.

300 **Ring your desk** with the home-run baseball you caught in the left-field stands at the World Series, with shells you collected on the best beach you ever visited, or with fossilized rocks you passionately collected in Ireland. Be willing to step into the unknown and decorate unconventionally; create the one cubicle in your building that is a shrine to just you.

301 **Bring childlike fascination** and wonder into your office. Hang from the ceiling your favorite dolls or GI Joes that you loved so much when you were ten. Or hang a beautiful box kite with a multi-colored tail, to remind you that you can still fly, even though you spend your days confined within four walls.

302 Create the comfort of your child-hood playroom, where adventure was hiding inside the cabinet, just under the couch, or right outside the door. Surround your desk blotter with all your favorite toys. Park die-cast metal model cars on your desk, including the 1969 Mustang fastback you always wanted, and a hook and ladder, in case there are any fires that you have to put out when clients call. Let these old toys remind you of the feeling that anything is possible, a feeling that seemed so natural when you played with toys like these as a kid.

303 Your first bicycle evokes memories of freedom and adventurous possibility. Hang a

picture of your first stingray, with banana seat and handlebar streamers. Or search for a Schwinn Apple Crate chopper on eBay, buy one, and lean it up against the outside of your cubicle. It will remind you that you're still free.

304 **Buy an old jukebox** and put it in your office to remind you that you can still dance. For about $1,000 you can buy a non-working Seeburg that lights up and evokes a simpler time. For $10,000, you can buy a restored Wurlitzer. For $10, you can buy a jukebox wall calendar.

305 **Buy the one thing** for your office that your parents would never allow in your childhood bedroom. If you always wanted a turtle with its own plastic palm tree, a Malibu Barbie, or a slot-car track, buy one. If you have no room for the slot-car track, buy a single piece of track and your favorite slot car at the hobby shop. Glue the car to the track and tape it on the partition that forms your cubicle. Be a child at your office and you'll be more available for adventures that come your way.

306 **Make a mini collage** of tiny photographs that depict you in your most adventurous moments: with best friends in a tree house or on a mountain summit, in an outrageous costume at a Halloween party, winning a blue ribbon at a horse show, or in front of the airport the first time you flew to Florida. Cover your collage in clear contact paper and post it in plain sight, on the edge of your computer monitor, next to the phone, or on the dashboard of the taxi you drive. Keep evidence of your adventurous spirit in plain view, so it will inspire you to be adventurous at work.

307 **Set up a portable stereo** and play your three favorite CDs randomly in the background. See if music opens up new territory as you grapple with the same old problems.

308 **Post pictures** in your office of the things you want to buy with the money you make at work. When you have a clear objective, your work will seem more adventurous, as you move closer and closer to your goals.

309 **Make your goals** into a visible adventure. Make a parchment treasure map (with burnt edges) and put your goals in the center. Color your financial progress on the trail to the buried treasure in the center, even if that treasure is braces for your kids or money for a new refrigerator.

310 **Get at least one plant** for your office. When it greets you with little buds one morning, your plant will remind you that every day is an adventure and you never know what to expect.

311 **Massage your stocking feet** on golf-ball and softball-size spiny massage balls while you work, and your feet will be warmed up for your next adventure. Leave them under your desk (two tennis balls work, too).

312 **Fill one drawer** in your desk with comfort food, creativity food, decadent food, and spicy-hot ginger candies. Have an arsenal of tastes available to help you manage your moods as they come and go and to fuel your body for your journey. Stock an inventory of herb teas. Perhaps a simple cup of tea will open your mind to new possibilities. Or maybe Tension Tamer will be useful the next time the boss throws a fit.

313 **Put some passion candles** on your credenza and light them when you need a big idea.

314 **Hang quotes,** cartoons, pictures of your heroes, and inspirational sayings all around your office.

315 **Put something you made** in your office. Display a painting, a photograph, a sculpture, or anything you made that makes you proud and reminds you of your creativity.

REQUEST

Requests always lead to adventures. You never know what kind of response you'll get. You may be tested and sent on a journey someplace new. Perhaps you'll be surprised to see the ease with which you can get what you need. Maybe you'll get rejected and better be able to see the way your associates value or don't value the contribution you make at work. Or maybe your request will bring out a life-altering compromise you hadn't even considered.

Learn to ask for what you want. It takes time and practice to be able to request everything you need. So start slowly. Make small requests at first, as you gain skill in flexing your new "requesting" muscle.

Even a job you hate can help you engage this adventure. You'll be happier, more productive, and more energized by your life if you ask for what you need. Your employer will reap the benefits. But more importantly, you'll evolve as a person and learn new skills you can use for the rest of your life, in every relationship. Step by step, request your way forward on your journey, sometimes like a climber trudging in the snow, at other times soaring along the mountain tops, but always continuing onward in your adventure while you sharpen your requests like your most precious sword.

316 **Ask for an improvement** to your physical office. Ask for a bigger desk that will help you to be more organized. Ask for your dirty walls to be painted your favorite color. Ask for a window to be installed so you can see the sun. Ask to make a garden of houseplants in your office. Ask for a better computer monitor. Ask for shelves or storage bins for your papers. Ask for anything that would fill your physical office with evidence that you are an honored employee of your company.

317 **Ask for one more thing.** Anything! Don't think that just because you asked for a new keyboard (because one of your Shift keys never worked) that you have used up your one coupon. For you, your adventure lives in the recognition that you really can ask for more. Requests are not annual events but part of an ongoing everyday practice. Don't just make one request and then retreat for another year.

318 **Ask for more service** from your company. Ask for the floor under your desk to be vacuumed every night. Ask to adjust your schedule so that you can commute when there is less traffic. Ask for a better parking space.

319 **Ask for opinions.** Ask your peers to tell you where they think you are on the request continuum. Are you whiney and demanding? Or are you a sheep who never speaks up? You don't have an objective opinion of where you fall on that continuum. Ask someone you trust.

320 **Ask to move offices** (or ask for an office) or ask if you can move to an area that has more natural light, if that would make you more effective in your work.

RELATE

Work brings infinite relationships into our lives. Imagine that you are going to the office today to get paid to be in relationship. Who might you meet today? When the phone rings at your desk, adventure is calling. Engage it. Listen attentively. Share something new. Take each relationship on an adventure into the unknown.

As you conduct your business today, get to know the people with whom you work. Celebrate the relationships all around you. The people you see every day are your companions on your adventure. Let them into your life. Acknowledge that they are no less adventurous than the people you would meet in a café in France or on a tour of a village in Thailand. It's not necessary to buy a plane ticket for your adventure; you can find all kinds of fascination simply by connecting with the people in your building and at the other end of your sales calls.

321 Spend a day focused on listening to everyone in your life. Listening is an

essential tool you'll need for your workplace adventures. You've stopped listening to certain people you see every day. Give them another chance. You just might be surprised that you meet familiar faces for the very first time. You might also discover that people around you have a lot to offer—more to offer than you ever realized.

322 Be a communication explorer.
Find out something intimate about the three people who work closest to you today. Don't pry into their personal affairs; simply find out their favorite color or their greatest dream.

323 Share yourself with your peers. Your
degree of self-expression is directly related to your job satisfaction. Tell someone in your office something personal today. Share your hobbies and your favorite places to travel. You work too hard keeping your vibrant personality a secret. Let it out and you'll discover new vitality.

324 **Design a regular forum** with your peers where you can chat about what's on your mind. Write a company e-newsletter. Organize a regular pizza party for all employees to be heard. Express yourself and you'll attract new relationships.

325 **Humanize your voice mail.** Be courageously willing to stand out. Let your voice mail be an energized expression of who you are. Call yourself and listen to your message. Does it sound like someone you'd want to meet? Or someone you would want to promote? Think of something you love and redo your message, so that your authentic and passionate self shines through.

326 **Get to know someone** in your office with whom you have never spoken. Get to know the janitors, ground workers, and delivery people, who all have interesting lives you can discover, if you stop to inquire. Because few people take the time, your interest is that much more special. You'll be surprised by the power of your connection and the possibilities for adventure that ensue.

327 Get to know your clients. Be genuinely interested in them and what they love to do in their free time. It's fun and good business. Find the person underneath that hard exterior. You might be surprised to discover that they have mastered origami or play the church organ with passion.

328 Share something intimate with one caller a day. I'm not talking about your romantic secrets. Tell them a story about your cat. Share something about your hobby. Tell them you just saw a great movie or read a great book. There are people all around you who can enhance the adventure of your workday. They have been waiting for you to come out and play.

329 **Call a new person every day.** Make contact with someone you respect or admire, even if you have no immediate business connection in mind.

330 **Exercise your courage** by reconnecting with someone you once knew. There are people in your network with whom you haven't been in contact for years. Call one of these people each day, just to see how they have been. You might discover that there is an adventure just waiting to unfold between you.

331 **Send someone** in your business community a personalized, handwritten note each week. Take the time to make your connections special and human once again. Each special relationship entitles you to journey deeper into unfamiliar space.

332 **Invite one of your coworkers** to do something active. Work out, run, bike, and sweat. Encourage one another to exercise. And take the relationship up a notch in the process.

333 **Repair a rift** with someone you're avoiding. When you have to hold up a shield against a particular person, it drains your resources. Practice forgiveness. You don't have to like everyone. But strive to be able to be in the company of everyone in your office. You'll find new energy when there is no one you have to plot to avoid.

Innovate

Your workday is an opportunity to explore the extent of your creativity, even if you are not paid to be creative. Think big and suggest something that would make your work more fun and exciting. You'll likely improve your company in the process.

Be innovative from the moment you get out of bed. Even if people in your company are not receptive to your creative contributions, your ability to innovate will make for an adventurous workday.

334 Strike a deal with a restaurant to provide a free tasting for your associates. Invite different local restaurants to bring their unique cuisine into your office each month. The restaurant will gain valuable exposure with new potential diners and you'll bring out new creativity in your office. Try sushi in January and goulash in February.

335 Hire a feng shui consultant to help you rearrange your office into its energetic best.

336 **Purchase beach ball–size** stretch balls for your conference room. Roll around on them once each day to loosen up your creativity.

337 **Get an office mascot or pet.** Adopt an office cat. Animals can alter the energy of your office, make your staff more human, and help unleash creativity hiding just beneath the surface.

338 **Hire a yoga teacher** to lead regular classes in your conference room, or a massage therapist, acupuncturist, chiropractor, or foot reflexologist to make a weekly visit.

339 **Become the company** greenhouse manager and fill a common space with green plants. If the company won't pay for them, maybe your coworkers will chip in, or everyone can bring one potted plant from home for a community "garden." (Be sure someone is signed on for watering.)

340 **Propose a reward structure** that matters more than money. Perhaps you want a chance to use the best parking spot. Or a coupon to come in late. Or a certificate for an extra half-hour for lunch. Suggest that performance could be rewarded with the perks that matter most to you and your peers. Create a new structure to reward your hard work, one that gives you what you need.

341 **Reward the best mistake.** People need to have the freedom to make mistakes if they are going to innovate.

342 **Create** a monthly or quarterly event that brings fun to your entire office. Try a scavenger hunt, softball game, indoor rock-climbing class, or nature walk. Charter a yacht and go for a company dinner cruise. Or rent a movie theatre to show an inspiring film. Perhaps a haunted-house tour on Halloween would energize your company. Or a weekend retreat at a ski, beach, fall-foliage, or mountaintop house. Organize an outing. Or a trip to the beach.

343 Hang a basketball hoop or volleyball net outside the office and play during lunch.

344 Drive to work on a different route. Leave five minutes earlier and appreciate the drive, rather than rushing through it. Add spice to your commute by taking your bike, or a train. Skate to work, carpool, or take a ferry if you can.

345 **Spend a day pretending** to be the person you admire most at work. How would they react to the situations that come your way?

346 **Find at least one pattern** in your workday that no longer serves you and interrupt it.

347 **Bring to work those ideas** you had in the shower. Even though the last idea fell on its face, this next one may change the world.

348 **Look at your whole day** with new eyes. Imagine that you are seeing your career for the first time. What would you change? Where would you innovate? Make a list of three ways your company can operate more efficiently and share it with someone who can actually implement your ideas.

349 **Spend your workday** backwards. Reverse your routine just to see if maybe you discover more energy.

350 **Explore life** as your own customer. Call or email and watch how your company works from the perspective of one of your customers. How long are you on hold? How long until you get a response? Use your discoveries to innovate.

CONTRIBUTE

Contribution will enliven your workday regardless of how you feel about your job. Someone in your department is waiting for you to give them love, support, information, or friendship. Your dull day can be full of fascination and wonder once you start to look for opportunities to contribute...and to be contributed to in the process. Once you focus on contribution, you eliminate the predictability of your daily routine. And even a job you hate becomes exciting when you focus on contribution and touch someone's life forever.

351 **Post letters from customers** throughout your office, to remind you of the contribution you make every day of the week. Ask customers for evidence of the contribution made by your product or service. Invite clients to send you examples of what they do with your product, to help you remain confident that your work has tremendous value. You make a difference with your presence and with your actions. Make that contribution visible to energize your day.

352 **Talk to your customers** when they call and let them contribute to you. Ask them how they feel about doing business with your company. They will appreciate the opportunity to give you feedback and will become more loyal in the process.

353 **Join an association** and give your time to support other professionals in your field. Share what you have learned with others who might benefit from the information.

354 **Become a mentor** for someone else who wants to get into your industry.

355 **Spend at least fifteen minutes** every day helping someone else get his or her job done flawlessly. Look for people in your office to inspire.

356 **Organize a volunteer program** for the company to give back to the community.

357 **Sponsor a Little League team**
through your company and offer to be one of the coaches.

SELF-DEVELOP

Whether you love your job or not, the adventure of self-development is forever yours to engage. There is so much to discover as you watch yourself navigate through the events that greet you on a simple day. Wherever you feel friction, you have a chance to probe deeper into your expectations. Every time you are challenged, you have the opportunity to leap through an open door and to learn something new about yourself.

Once you see your personal growth as a delicious bonus that's available on a daily basis, you have the luxury of gaining strength from an otherwise ordinary day at work. People have been invigorated by their financial and material victories for years, in spite of the fact that such achievements are temporary. Your personal victories are yours for life. Let these victories permeate and energize your entire body, as you embrace this wondrous adventure of everyday life.

358 **Chances are good** that you have a list of things or people who bother you at your job. One by one, look at the people on your list and consider that maybe the people who bug you mirror something you hate about yourself. Those coworkers are actually teachers who can support you on your journey to evolve as a human being.

359 **Shift your focus** to self-discovery. If you hate your job, you're probably fixated on what your employer doesn't provide. It may not change. But you have the power to change yourself. Ask for feedback at least once each week. Listen to the comments of your managers and peers; work to evolve.

360 **Find a mentor** who can be your partner as you move through your career. Hire a coach, find a retired executive from your industry, or listen to any wise advisor who can help you clearly see opportunities for growth.

361 **Learn the art of saying "no."** You win no awards for being overworked. Learn to decline without making it mean that there is something deficient about you. Practice declining with grace by saying "no" to one thing every day for a week.

362 **Make self-development** an ongoing exercise. Read at least one book about self-exploration every month. Attend at least one lecture, seminar, or workshop that will further your personal journey.

363 **Become a leader** for self-development in your firm. Create an informal lending library in your office of personal growth and self-help titles. Offer to bring training and lectures to your company that will support you and your peers on your voyage of discovery.

364 **Let go** of at least one complaint about your workplace each week. You may be right about a number of things that could be improved. But struggling with issues over which you have no control taxes your vitality. Focus on what you can control. Practice letting go. If necessary, find a new company that values your contribution.

365 **Dive into a project** at work—one that's been waiting for someone to get around to, or that no one else wants to do. Even if you fail, you'll strengthen useful muscles in the process.

366

Admit a mistake and make amends. It takes great courage to apologize. Afterwards, you'll feel one thousand pounds lighter.

career

LIFE WITH ARCHIE

My grandfather had a thing for Betty and Veronica. In 1941, he and his partner founded Archie Comics. My father and the son of my grandfather's partner have owned the company since 1982. I worked for them for nine years marketing the characters in new venues. I orchestrated fast-food promotions, new cartoons, and Archie movie ventures. I enjoyed the sheer entrepreneurial opportunity of the job. And my Archie days provided lots of funny stories that could even stand alone in their own comic book. But, frankly, there was so much friction between my father, his partner, and me that life at Pops's Chocklit Shoppe was often a real drag. We all had strong wills, as well as different outlooks for what was possible with the Archie characters.

In 1993, at the age of thirty-two and at the height of a lousy job market, I walked away from it all. At what could have been called the apex of my career, I left, dissatisfied with the predictable future that lay before me. I knew how it would turn out if I stayed at Archie. I'd spend my life in a permanent argument with my dad and his partner, just as they had with their dads, as I waited for my turn to run the business. In spite of the financial security I had that so many people covet, I found the environment oppressive. So I quit. I had no shares in the business and no trust funds. My dad made it clear that leaving meant no inheritance either. But none of that stopped me. I wasn't willing to give my life to Archie for any amount of money in the world.

In many ways, my departure from the family business was the beginning of my biggest adventure. I felt like I risked my life when I left a known future for a future that was unknown in every way.

But in the years that followed, I discovered that I could in fact create a business that was completely based on my own unique skills. I studied coaching and built a coaching practice to support people to make life choices, like the one I had made, in the name of authenticity and adventure. It often seems that money corrupts this choice and that money becomes the primary motivator for life choices in general. But I found in my own life and in the lives of my clients that money seems to flow to people who make authenticity and adventure integral to everything they do.

When I took my career into my own hands, I discovered that this was the path to prosperity in every arena of my life. I also discovered that the only place where security exists is in a career that allows people to do what they love most. Even though I haven't yet eclipsed my earnings at Archie, I always have enough to do what I want in my life. Meanwhile, I love the fact that my coaching work makes a measurable difference in people's lives. Every client is on a different adventure, and I feel privileged to be invited along.

I have no regrets about leaving the family business. I'm grateful for the chance I had to discover that adventure, not money, defines me. Funny that I had to leave a comic-book company in order to find out just how much fun work can be.

adventures
with
(and without)
money

The financial world seems devoid of adventure unless you have a reserve of cash. Only those with extra money can play. Everyone else is forced to use their money for survival. I use the term survival very loosely; whether you need every dollar to eat or you struggle to earn enough so you can send your kids to private school, there is little freedom with how you spend your money. Many people live with an incessant flow of expenses that seems to devour anything they make, regardless of their income level. Adventure never even seems like a possibility.

We tend to be overly reductive about money. We perceive it in one of two ways: we either have it or we don't. And so we are often stuck in our relationship with money. We compulsively earn it, spend it, rebel against it, or hoard it. But we have little freedom to experience any adventure with it. We are gripped by money, and from this place, it's very difficult to get out from under any financial burdens or to experience any sense of financial abundance. Only when we challenge our relationship with money and loosen our grip on it does money loosen its grip on us.

And that's why money represents such a wonderful adventure. There is a vast opportunity to explore far beyond the status-quo relationship that normally defines our struggles with money. Money is actually like a vast ocean, with infinite features to explore.

To simply unravel your preconceived notions about money is a great adventure. There is so much to discover as you uncover your habits and denial about money. Once you can fully identify your automatic behaviors, you then have the freedom to actually have a relationship with money that gives you power, instead of haphazardly repeating the past.

For generations we have made cash "king." We have surrendered our power to a symbol of wealth and let money be our master. But when you reclaim your own power, you become the master of money and it starts to become no different than any other tool you effectively use in your everyday life.

We are well skilled at blaming money for everything that works or doesn't work in our lives. Little by little you can unravel this blame and open up a new relationship that leaves money in its rightful place as nothing more than paper and metal we have designated for the sole purpose of exchange.

The purpose of this chapter is to expand your thinking about money. Strive for an ongoing opening in your relationship with money, where each day you might discover something new. Discover the freedom you have to live your life without being ruled by money. Regardless of how much you make or spend, explore the possibility that you can develop a new relationship with money where you control it and it doesn't control you.

PLAY WITH MONEY

We tend to approach money as though it was essential to our survival, like oxygen, and we would die if we altered the relationship it has to our lives. Such an attitude limits what you can create with money. Once you can play with it, you have the ability to be free. Don't be reckless with money. But when you challenge the strict relationship you might have had with money, you open yourself up to fun and adventure in a domain that will forever be a component of everyday life.

367 **Create a wide-open space** in your wallet. Make more room for money in your life. Clean out all the assorted junk that obliterates any space that might otherwise be filled with cash. Get a second photo wallet if you must carry pictures of all your relatives and discount cards from all the mass merchandisers. But make sure that you have an elegant wallet that makes you feel rich, with ample room to receive abundant amounts of cash.

368 **Make your wallet sacred.** Honor every bill that enters your life. Organize each one perfectly, in numerical order, all facing the same direction. Stop crumpling bills and randomly leaving them in every pocket. Keep a meticulous wallet for a month and see if you discover new respect for your money.

369 **Devise a system** that guarantees that your wallet will always be with you. Make your wallet part of your daily adventure gear. Carry it like a multi-tool or a cell phone clipped to your belt, ready for immediate deployment. Invest in a fanny pack, money belt, or suitable holster, so that your money is always ready for your next adventure. You can't have any power with money until you have a structure to keep your wallet with you at all times.

370 **Carry more cash.** When you have $50 or $100 or $200 in your wallet at all times, you have more flexibility and power to engage adventures that come your way. Get larger amounts of money on visits to the ATM, so that lack of funds is no longer an excuse when you are invited to play.

371 **Cash your next paycheck** in one-dollar bills. Spend a week paying for everything with singles. Have fun peeling off bills from a giant wad. Money loses its meaning when you charge everything and pay with a monthly check to your credit-card company. Have a tactile adventure with your money; both you and the vendor will discover something new when you handle it in every transaction.

372 **Give monetary gifts** and bonuses in one-dollar bills. When you give someone a check, the gift has impact only when it is first revealed. The perceived value of the gift quickly fades when that money is deposited. But a stack of crisp, new, banded singles feels like a weighty gift. The recipient can carry and spend the singles throughout their day. This way, your monetary gift will travel with them, the same way jewels or gold would travel with a medieval explorer.

373 **Go to a stationery store** or print shop with a stack of crisp new five-, ten-, or twenty-dollar bills and ask them to make it into a pad by smearing glue on one edge. Tear them off individually as you run your errands to make the process of dispensing your money novel and fun.

374 **Leave your credit cards** at home for just one weekend. Fill your wallet with a fixed amount of cash and spend no more than what you put in your wallet. Credit cards give us the illusion that our funds are infinite. Explore what it used to be like before you got credit cards, when you had a clear sense of how much you had and how much you could spend.

375 **Make art out of money.** Create a collage of various bills. Or dollar origami. Or pin crisp new singles end to end around your bedroom to make a monetary crown molding. With a photocopier, enlarge the faces of the dignitaries on each bill. Hand-color them and create a gallery of fiscal portraits.

Make Christmas ornaments from dollar bills. Challenge your fear to leave money out in the open. Get creative with money and you'll discover new freedom to use it for creative expression in every area of your life.

376 Collect unique currency. Ask friends to bring you back a $1 equivalent from every country in the world. Display the varied symbols used for legal tender. Or collect each of the commemorative American quarters, one from every state, and display them in a decorative U.S. map holder, which you can buy in bookstores. Put money on display and you'll start to feel rich.

377 Cash your next paycheck in $20 bills and hide one in every pant and coat pocket, so that you constantly surprise yourself with little monetary gifts.

378

Visit the United States mint and watch money being printed. See if money loses some of its meaning when you see that it is printed on a press, just like any other paper product. Or perhaps it will gain more significance, as you watch the way it is so carefully protected. Ask to see printing mistakes; buy some one-sided dollar bills. Deepen your relationship with money; watch it being born.

379

Give away ten singles in a day. Give a dollar to the first person to compliment you. Ask someone for a solution to a problem. The reward? One dollar. Try to give a stranger a dollar, no strings attached. Tie a string to a dollar and leave it under someone's desk at work. See what they will do as you pull it just out of reach. Tape a few singles to trees that grow along your city sidewalks and watch to see how long it takes for people to notice. Who knows what you may start; once people start to think that money grows on trees, perhaps more trees will be planted in your city!

380 **Discover the power** of a single dollar in a money game with a group of friends. Hold up a dollar and see who has something to provide in exchange, whether it's a foot rub, a palm reading, or relationship advice. Whoever gets the dollar makes the same offer to the group and exchanges that same dollar for another service or product. Let the dollar travel around the entire group, with each person buying and selling. Notice how freely commerce evolves. Strive to make buying and selling effortless in your daily routine.

381 **Charge your friends and family** for repeat violations of those things that make you angry. Make it clear that late arrivals will be billed at $1 per minute and failure to return phone calls within forty-eight hours carries a $5 penalty. Don't use this as an opportunity to create hostility and tension; instead, make this into a game that reveals your frustrations and simultaneously provides financial reward when

people let you down. Charge one dollar in advance for every idea that you dispense. Use this structure to better value what you contribute to the world. As you practice asking people for money for the service you provide, you'll ultimately make it easier the next time you need to ask for a raise.

382 Write a note on a dollar bill and see if it comes back to you. Put a few dollars in a clear bottle and set it adrift, with a note inviting whoever finds it to use the money to call you once they receive it.

383 Surround yourself with representations of money. Buy tissues printed to look like dollar bills. Wear ties and shirts imprinted with bills. Make a money screen saver and mouse pad. Tape dollar bills on the leaves of a houseplant. Buy dollar-sign pajamas and see if anything new happens once you look like

Richie Rich. Put evidence of money out in the open. Stop denying that money is part of your life.

384 **Surprise your spouse** and periodically hide money under their pillow, like a tooth fairy for adults.

385 **Scatter all your change** throughout your car, so that it covers the floors, seats, and dashboard. Regardless of the quality of your vehicle, you'll drive in luxury, knowing that there is plenty of money to go around.

386 **Hide a small amount of money** throughout your home in every secret nook and cranny. Hide enough so that you forget exactly where it's all hidden and you'll constantly find money while cleaning your home.

387 **Reward yourself** for knowing where to find wisdom. The next time you read an inspirational passage in a book you love, bookmark it with a monetary gift. The next time you read the passage, take the cash that marked the appropriate page.

388 **Give a great birthday gift** that costs you no money. Make a coupon book that entitles the recipient to various things they enjoy, like a night at the movies, a back rub, dishes washed, a walk in the moonlight, or a passionate kiss. Or give a coupon book to your child for their birthday, filled with pages that allow them to stay up late, rent multiple videos, invite friends for sleepovers, and get rides across town.

389 **Make no purchases** for an entire week. Just for fun, see if you can use what you already have in your life without consuming anything new. Resist the urge to run out and buy the latest and greatest gadget. Make do with what you have. You might even find more time for adventures around your home once you stop running into town every day to shop.

GIVE AWAY MONEY

Giving away money is always an adventure since you never know what, if anything, will come back to you. Every time you give some away, you acknowledge that you have the power to make more. You also endorse a deep belief that there will always be ample money in your life.

It's often the people who don't actually have a lot of money who are masterful at giving it away. They seem to focus on making "enough" money, not "a lot" of money. With the latter attitude, no amount earned is ever enough, and there is rarely any to give away. But when you are committed to having enough, you are free from the insatiable desire to make more. And you are free to touch others with a monetary gift, often just for the adventure of it.

390 **Randomly give** small anonymous gifts to strangers, simply to loosen up the hold that money has on your life. Pay the highway toll for the car behind you. Leave one dollar inside a returned library book. Fold a dollar bill over a box of Lucky Charms cereal in the supermarket, so that a child who grabs the box will wonder if leprechauns are actually real. Leave a $1 bill in the tube that greets the next car at the bank drive-up window, along with a small note that says today is their lucky day. You might even find that more money comes back to you than what you give away.

391 **Be a contemporary** Robin Hood. Budget $100 each year to anonymously endorse your values. When you see someone propose marriage in a restaurant, buy the couple dessert, so that you can privately participate in their joyous celebration. If you see a father and son bonding over lunch, buy it for them, to endorse the intimacy you may not have had with your parents. When you see a child crying in a store

235

because his older brother took his candy, give the younger boy a few dollars so he can buy his own, just because your brother used to take your candy, too.

392 Donate money for a scholarship fund, so that someone without financial means can learn something that made a difference in your life. Don't just give away what's left over when you die. Give your money away while you are still alive. Enjoy watching the difference you can make. Regardless of your income, give away at least 2 percent of what you make every year to people who need it more than you do.

393 Make tipping an adventurous ceremony. Don't just give people tips because you are afraid to look cheap. Actually use tipping as an acknowledgment of the person who provided service. Look them in the eyes and thank them for a job well done. Stop leaving your tips on your credit-card receipt and dashing out of the restaurant without thanking your server. Look them in the eye; tell them that you left them an acknowledgment of the service they provided. Or tip people in cash, just for the sheer value of making the ritual real instead of some anonymous formality. Be responsible for what you tip, high or low, and walk away in freedom.

394 Be generous. Tip at least one person a year $20 where a dollar would be appropriate. In that moment, you will really be someone important in the mind of the recipient, and for $20, that's a bargain.

395 Fill your house with a wacky piggy-bank collection acquired at garage sales and thrift stores. Put one next to your kitchen sink and deposit twenty-five cents each time you do the dishes. Put two in your bathroom and put a dollar in one each

time you floss and a dime in another each time you flush. When you wash your car, deposit $5 in the bank in your garage, and when you vacuum, deposit $10 in the bank in your utility closet. Every year, have a giving adventure by handing the fund to someone in need.

396 **Pay everyone back** from whom you ever borrowed money. Go back as far as you can remember. Search the Internet for old high school buddies from whom you borrowed $20 and mail them an unexpected gift. Even give money back to the people who never expected to be paid back.

397 **Give adventurous monetary** gifts in your family. On birthdays, multiply the person's age by one, five, or ten dollars and give that amount annually to your children. Or use that structure to give money back to your parents, to honor what they gave you when you were a kid. Give people lottery tickets for their birthday, too; perhaps you will make someone a millionaire.

398 **Hold a tag sale** every year to turn unused items into cash. Use the proceeds to make a difference in your community. Donate the money to a local charity.

399 **Get a toll-free number.** When you travel, give this number to new friends with whom you want to stay in touch. Invite them to call you once each year to reminisce and to keep your adventures alive. Also give this number to any friends who use lack of funds as an excuse for not calling. Many phone companies can add this service to your existing phone line for a small fee.

400 Silence parental money whining. When you're together, pay for lunch, dinner, museums, movies, gas, or whatever they complain has gotten too expensive. Even if you have to budget an annual amount for this expense, it's well worth the price to have some peace together. Consider this expense an investment in a relationship adventure. Once their money babble is off the table, there might be some space to talk about something that matters, other than the fact that phone calls used to cost just a nickel.

401 Give to every panhandler that crosses your path. Budget $50 every year and give one dollar to everyone who asks you for money instead of looking the other way and ignoring them. Stop being suspicious about whether they are legitimately in need. Simply give them what they ask for.

402 **Encourage your kids** to be junior philanthropists. Give them an appropriate amount every year that they have to give away. Encourage them to explore the world of difference-making opportunities and to choose a cause they want to impact directly.

403 **Make a will.** Deal with the reality that you are only borrowing your own money for your lifetime, and when you die, it will go to someone else. If you don't have a will, you haven't accepted the fact that your finances are just temporary. Let go of the notion that you can hold on to your money even after you die.

ATTITUDE

You probably learned your attitude about money from your parents. Whether they struggled with money or were sloppy with their finances, chances are good that you either inherited their attitude about money or continue to rebel against their attitude about money. Either way, you're stuck in a box, with little freedom to truly explore an adventurous relationship with your finances.

Your parents formed their opinions about money in radically different times. Let go of the perspective that was handed down to you. Declare your independence from the money voices that are not your own. Challenge what you have always thought was true about money and create a new adventurous perspective that is uniquely yours.

404

Explore what it will take to feel financially rich. Define the exact salary that would result in your financial freedom. Create concrete goals, whether you hope to make twenty-five thousand or twenty-five million every year. Many people have a vague goal simply defined as "making more" or "making millions." If you don't have a specific target, you can never feel financially fulfilled.

405 **Become more intimate** with your money. No matter where you are financially, take your relationship to a new level. Meet with an expert and design a financial plan. Balance your checkbook. Or if your credit-card debt exceeds your annual income, declare bankruptcy. Take your relationship with money from one of denial to one of intimacy. Once you have a clear picture of your financial reality, you can start to interact with money from a place of power.

406 **Accept all money** that is offered to you. Stop offering to pay for a meal when someone else picks up the check. Stop trying to look like a hero because you offered to pay. Stop trying to be polite and turn down money that you are offered. Accept it. Welcome it. Be grateful for it. And perhaps you will find that even more money will start to flow your way.

407 **Pay your taxes** before the end of January. Don't waste any energy carrying unpaid taxes through an entire quarter of your year. Discover how much less stress the process has if you pay promptly, get your refund promptly, pay your accountant for the service promptly, and move on to a new financial year by February 1st.

408 **Explore a debt-free lifestyle.** Strive to pay off everything so that money loses its hold over you. At the very least, spend twelve months with no credit-card balance. You might be surprised to discover that paying off your debt opens up space for more money to flow into your life.

409 **Photocopy big checks** that you get for your most creative work and pin them on the wall. That $200 you got for your World Series baseball or $10,000 you got for your first consulting project is long gone, buried in your bank balance. But the copy of the check is timeless, and stuck on your refrigerator door, it will remind you of the power you have to make amazing amounts of money for doing relatively simple things.

410 **Commit to a charity event** that requires you to raise an unreasonable amount of money. Use the event as an opportunity to explore your relationship to discussing money with strangers. You'll be surprised to find that people welcome an opportunity to contribute money to a worthwhile cause. If you are raising money for a charity walk or bike ride, people will also enjoy living vicariously through you with their contribution.

411 **Explore the possibility** that your persistent lower-back pain is directly linked to your fearful attitude about money. Find a way to pad your lower back with two one hundred–dollar bills. Pin them to the inside of your shirt. Sew two pockets into your favorite T-shirt. Or invest in a bicycling jersey, which has back pockets. Carry the money over your pain. The bills will act like splints to support you and to alleviate some of the burden normally carried on your back.

412 Become a money expert. Listen to personal-finance radio shows in your car. Borrow books about money from the library. Study the psychology of money. People sometimes think that studying money makes them greedy or shallow. But financial education gives you power. Explore the topic with a sense of adventure.

SPEND, SAVE, EARN

People are often good at spending, saving, or making money, but rarely are they good at all three. Explore each discipline fully. Move deep into each domain and fully experience what it's like in each of these distinct worlds.

Once you have equal freedom to spend, save, and earn money, you'll discover that money is no longer a source of friction in your life.

You probably have a strong opinion about your particular methods with money. That very opinion is what likely closes off any adventure. Attack the stuck areas of your monetary life with abandon and you'll discover that you have a world of "shoulds" about money that you never even knew existed. Your exploration of each financial arena where freedom is missing can transform your stale and automatic relationship with money into an exciting adventure.

SPENDING ADVENTURES

413 **Set up an adventurous system** to manage your bills. Pay all monthly bills under $100 quarterly, in advance. Each check you write costs you time and energy. Each bill you receive that needs to be paid is a distraction from your everyday adventures. Try to only think about paying bills four times each year.

You should also use online banking to schedule automatic payments for recurring monthly bills and carry a credit balance with the phone company. That way, you can throw away your phone bills each month (after you review them) until the credit balance reaches zero.

414 Look for other ways to provide value. When money stops you from participating in something you want to do, ask what you can provide instead. Money is not the only thing the seller needs. Offer to wash airplanes if you can't afford flying lessons. Trade your labor or your skill for something you would otherwise not be able to afford. You have something that the seller wants. When money stops you, your job is to find out what that is and to see if you can provide it. Money is simply a tool to facilitate an exchange. Find another way to make exchange possible.

415 **Give yourself an outrageous** gift every birthday. Purchase a tangible acknowledgment of another year of hard work, like a new car, a watch, a piece of jewelry, or a piece of furniture. Turn the money you made into something real that you see every day. Otherwise, your earnings only exist on paper.

416 **Don't wait** until retirement age to give yourself what you've always wanted. Give yourself at least one big present every decade. If you want a boat, don't wait until you lack the energy to enjoy it. If you dream of someday owning a potter's wheel, a complete woodshop, or a greenhouse, invest in it now. Your hobbies feed your health and well-being. Splurge on them today, so you can celebrate the adventure of your everyday life right now, rather than waiting until you reach age sixty-five. If you don't have the budget for such luxury items, search the classifieds for bargains.

417 Protest with pennies.

If you think your property taxes are too high, pay them in pennies. Call the local paper and have them meet you at the tax collector's office as you deliver a truckload of coins. Maybe the press coverage will open a debate about what is fair for all residents. If nothing else, you will use your money artfully, rather than complaining for another year without making your objections known to someone who can do something about it.

418 Visit the land of list prices.

Stop wasting time comparison shopping for something that you will use for hundreds of hours. One hundred dollars saved on a stereo computes to fractions of a penny saved per song. Five hundred dollars saved on a car purchase computes to a penny per mile for every fifty thousand miles driven. It's great to save money, especially when you don't have it, but your time is more precious. Use the time you would spend chasing the best price to make a lot more money than what you might save.

419 **Take control** over store coupons. They are marketing tools designed to get you to visit a store when you otherwise wouldn't or to make you buy more than you would buy without them. Discover what it's like to only use them for purchases you would have made anyway.

420 **Give yourself a gift certificate** at your favorite store or catalog. Post the actual printed certificate on your refrigerator and triumphantly spend it when you have cause to celebrate. You'll experience a greater joy in spending that certificate than you would if you were to simply buy what you want off the shelf. You can also use gift certificates to help you budget your hobby expenses; for example, you could buy six $100 certificates and commit to spending no more throughout the year.

421 **Eradicate useless gifts** from your life. Give your spouse, best friend, or family a wish list at least once each year. No one will ever again wonder what to get you as a gift, and you'll make it easy for people to shop for you. Even a wish list of books you want to read can make your next holiday season particularly rewarding.

Saving Adventures

422 **Buy used goods.** There is an entire world of bargain newspapers and Internet sites to explore where you can locate exactly what you want for less money. Make sure you get help with anything motorized, since poor maintenance by the former owner could lessen the product's life span. But used CDs, barbecues, and bicycles are seldom worn out when they are put on sale. You might also enjoy meeting the former owner of the used products you purchase so that you can hear the adventurous history of the items you buy.

423 **Fill a giant water-cooler** bottle to the brim with the daily change from your pockets. Empty your coins nightly into this giant, transparent piggy bank. Then hold a competition with your friends to guess the amount inside. Cash in the coins and take your pals for a great night out with the proceeds. Or use them for a trip to Mexico or a down payment on a car.

424 **Ask for a discount.** Designate one photo store as the exclusive shop for all your film and processing. Offer one dry cleaner the exclusive on all your business. Offer to make your auto mechanic the exclusive keeper of your cars. And be courageous enough to ask for a 10 percent discount on all your purchases as a reward for that loyalty. If you like the service you receive, reward the vendor with a holiday gift equal to the amount you saved. In this way, your mundane relationships with everyday vendors become adventurous games.

425 **Each time you write a check,** think about rounding the amount up to the nearest $10 increment. Take that small sum and put it away in your savings account. Use the money to take a vacation or pursue a hobby.

Earning Adventures

426 **Ask for a raise.** You'll have an adventure if you can ask without making the process so self-important. Just asking may be all it takes to get what you want. And if you get rejected, have the freedom to let that be insignificant too. Be a compensation archaeologist. Dig until you find out what it would take for you to earn more money in your company. Seek to provide it.

427 **Ask for more money** for the services you provide, if you're self-employed. Even if you lose some customers, offer the best service and charge more for it. Have the courage to declare yourself a premium provider. Explore that new identity. You'll discover that clients often put more value on a service when you charge more for it.

428 Hold a garage sale specifically to raise money for a cause that moves you. It could be for a charity, for your own vacation in New Zealand, or to build an addition on your house. People will rally to support you once they know where their money is going.

429 Make something yourself and sell it at a craft fair. For about $30, you can rent space at a local church festival. Or hold your own craft fair on your front lawn, and invite your neighbors. Charge 20 percent more money for each item than what you think they are worth. You'll be pleasantly surprised to see that your work really is worth it.

430 **Sell something** that has been sitting in your house unused. Perhaps the treadmill you bought from the home-shopping channel is still in the box. Or maybe your old computer still has enough power to be useful for someone else. There is something in your garage or basement that has value. List it in the classifieds today.

431 **Ask for financial assistance** instead of complaining about the things you can't afford. If you can't afford a course in website design, ask if scholarships are available. If you want to get a degree at an expensive institution, ask for financial aid. If you are a struggling artist, ask the state for an individual artist's grant. Often, money is a barrier only if you are unwilling to ask for relief.

432 **Offer to save people money** by doing something you love for less than what they would otherwise have to pay. Do this work one day each month and build a special savings fund for something you always wanted. You already have skills for which you can charge money. Your adventure lies in asking people to pay you for it. Put up a flyer in your neighborhood offering your product or service, and that way, interested parties will come to you.

433 **Sell trash.** Place classifieds in the back of magazines to sell your collection of back issues that you would otherwise dump in the recycle bin. Sell as firewood fallen trees that would otherwise end up in the landfill. Sell parts from old machines that you would otherwise throw in the dumpster. Use eBay to sell items that you would otherwise discard.

THE MONEY ANGEL

My friend Marta has a friend, we'll call her Jane, who wanted to go home and be with her parents for Christmas but couldn't afford it. So Marta bought a cheap airline ticket from a ticket agent who agreed to send it to Jane without any indication of who had paid for it.

What makes this story particularly special is that Marta is not a wealthy woman. She owns a car and a small business and not much else. She's thirty years old and instead of spending all her money or saving it for her future, she likes to spend some of it to surprise the people she loves. She periodically hides a hundred-dollar bill in a friend's purse or bedroom when she hears that they are struggling with bills or wedding expenses. And she always remains anonymous and seeks no credit for her gifts. She simply wants to give her friends something to make a difference in their lives. She's a real-life tooth fairy, for adults.

One day, Jane called Marta, ecstatic. "You'll never guess what my parents did. They sent me an anonymous ticket home for Christmas. And they're so cute, they already sent me my gifts, so that I wouldn't suspect that the ticket came from them."

Marta did a convincing job of sounding amazed by the story.

The next day, Jane called again. "It wasn't my parents. It must have been Rebecca. I can't believe she would do this for me. Isn't that awesome?"

And the next day, "It wasn't Rebecca! Was it you? Nah, no way you could afford this."

To this day, Jane hasn't figured it out.

For the price of a $249 plane ticket, Marta bought Jane and herself a money adventure that will last a lifetime.

the
adventure
of
nature

Nature is full of adventurous mysteries. The overcast layer you might have dismissed as just plain "cloudy" can show you so much more when you examine it with adventurous eyes and discover that it's alive. The ugly bug you were about to flatten is actually a living piece of artwork, if you get down on your knees and take a closer look at its magical locomotion and camouflage color scheme. Peak fall foliage weekend is not the only time to notice trees; the unfolding foliage in the spring is every bit as exciting. And airflow in your life should not just be limited to switching from norm to max in your car on the way to work. Air moves horizontally and vertically in nature in a constant magical dance, which you can actually see when you know what to look for. Everywhere you look, nature offers an opportunity for adventurous discovery and deep and profound connection.

But we live as though we are separate from the natural world, and then we spend our lives longing for connection. We are all made of the same stuff. If we would simply welcome a deep relationship with nature, we would find the profound spiritual fulfillment that we seek. Each natural adventure is an opportunity to bond with the natural world and thus find a new connection with our higher self.

In such uncertain times when we never know what will happen next, nature demonstrates mastery in the face of change. Nature shows us how to find the present moment, because more weather and new seasons are always just around the corner. The most beautiful flower has just a few days to remain in full bloom, yet there seems to be no problem with this in nature. Through the movement of time and the passage of seasons, nature shows us how to take change in stride.

On the surface, your local natural surroundings may not seem sufficiently exciting and adventurous. Perhaps you have shut off your senses and long for "real" adventure elsewhere. As a result, you may be missing the precious quality of the river that flows through town because it lacks a fifty-foot waterfall. And you'll never hike to the top of the highest hill in your town because no one was ever credited with the first ascent. You may have put adventure into a box reserved for people who travel to the ends of the Earth to witness nature's peak experiences. Actually, people who can find natural adventure in their own neighborhood are the most adventurous. Their spirit transcends their location and circumstances.

Natural adventures are available to everyone, regardless of income or vacation time. No expensive equipment or training is required. All you need is a willingness to look out the window with adventurous eyes. And for the rest of your life, nature will delight you with surprises on a daily basis.

EARTH ADVENTURES

Get to know the rock on which you live. We tend to seek our adventures somewhere out there, in a place where we are not. But right beneath the soles of your shoes, there's a world to explore. Look downward. Learn about the foundation on which you stand. You don't need a course in geology. But, some basic exploration of the geological history of your surroundings will give you a new perspective. Learn something about the hill you climb every day on your way to work, or the basic composition of the soil in your backyard.

434 Explore the Grand Canyon on your daily commute. Pull over to the shoulder and study the rock that was cut when your local roads were built. Notice the layers in the blasted or cut rock. Slow down and imagine that you are floating past in a rubber raft. Each layer tells a story about a time period every bit as significant and exciting as our layer of sediment that will be laid on top. Look at the striations. These are the layers of sediment that have been laid down for generations before the birth of the automobile. Sediment is always laid down horizontally. Vertical layers tell you that intense natural forces caused the folds. Intrusions are dramatic stripes of formerly molten rock that flowed into cracks. Every road cut tells a story. Learn to read it.

435 **Pick up at least one rock** every day and scan it for interesting features. Look for unusual crystals. Search for clear bits of mica embedded in stones that sparkle, which you can peel off, like little chips of clear plastic. A white stripe in a stone is often a piece of once-hot magma. You're holding part of a jigsaw puzzle; your local stones were part of a larger layer of rock before they broke off. Get to know the predominant makeup of the stones that surround your house, so you better understand what formed the foundation upon which you live.

436 **Be like a kid** and question the natural features surrounding your home. How did those boulders arrive in your backyard? What made the hill on which your house sits? How long has the stream flowed through your property? Head to the library and look for books on your local geology. You may not make it to Yosemite this year, but at least you can discover what made the valley that surrounds your house and how the body of water on the edge of town was formed.

437 **Mark magnetic north** on your property to anchor yourself in relation to the Earth's magnetic field. Even though it's not the same as scrambling through the wilderness with a GPS, you need your bearings at home, too. North is the reference point without which your home is lost on its adventure. No matter where you live, just knowing the direction of the North Pole makes you more adventurous.

438 **Get high.** Mark the highest point on your property with a flag or a lawn chair and return there frequently, to see what you can discover from this new perspective. Get to the top of your office building, even if you have to get to know the security guard and invite yourself up with him the next time he needs to inspect the roof. Find the highest point in your city. Climb the mountain or observation tower outside of town, just to see if you can find your home in the valley below. Look down on your town like a pilot preparing to make a landing.

439 Get low. Find the lowest part of your property and your town. Call the local historical society and ask if there are any catacombs underneath your town hall. Go on a tour of the mine outside of town. Explore the local cave system. Ask the road repairmen if you can have a peek inside their manhole. Get a topographical map of your town at the library and look for the lowest point. Go there and see if you discover anything new.

440 Fall in love with a field. Find an expanse of green or brown field and go to the center, just to feel the pure reserve of space. Appreciate the wide-open ocean of earth all around you,

nature

where you can finally think without the clutter of your daily life. Out in your field, perhaps you will begin to see your life with new clarity, unobstructed by your normal circumstances. Lie in the exact middle and look at the sky. Take your lover there for an evening picnic. Go there often, when life seems too complicated, and celebrate your secret affair with your field.

441 **Celebrate dirt.** You've driven past hundreds of "boring" plowed farmers' fields without even acknowledging them. Stop your car and meet one today. For a deeper adventure, go barefoot and feel the earth squish between your toes. Somewhere in that field lives the power to produce our crops. Can you feel any energy in the dirt?

442 **Start your day with fruit.** Eat an assortment of fresh fruit in season for breakfast at least one day each week. If it's local fruit, or

homegrown, so much the better. Peel or cut it yourself (fruit salad from the store or canned fruit won't do) and notice the direct connection you have with the earth, from the soil to the branch of the grapefruit tree directly to your kitchen, with no processing or packaging other than what nature provides. No matter how urban your environment, let your morning fruit transport you to endless orange groves in Florida or to a giant banana plantation in Belize. As your body harnesses the energy inside this fruit, it is the energy of that pristine environment that will power you through your day.

443 **Narrow the gap** between the beautiful fruit that started your day and the beautiful people who cross your path throughout your day. Just as you acknowledged the beauty of the fruit you ate as a perfect product of the earth, look for that same magic quality in the people you see. Try to find a new interpretation for everyone, including your boss.

444

Follow whatever leaves your house on its journey back to the earth. Visit your local water-treatment plant to see where water goes once it goes down your drain. Tour your local trash facility. Find out if your garbage is buried in a landfill or burned to make energy. Visit your local recycling plant and watch them sort the material you put out on the curb. Tours are usually free. Bring the kids on this adventure of discovery. Once you understand the wild ride your trash experiences once it leaves your home, taking out the trash will never be the same.

445

Discover nature's garbage. Scan every branch for old bird nests, empty bee-hives, and vacant cocoons. Look for snake skins and fallen deer antlers (they shed every winter). Even animal droppings can tell you exactly who lives in your neighborhood. A pile of feathers tells a story of a former pigeon, perhaps killed by a peregrine falcon or a red-tailed hawk.

446 **Take a walk in the woods** and scan the earth for clues. Get to know the difference between fox, coyote, and opossum tracks. Paw prints may lead to a family of raccoons spending a day in a tree. Stop and investigate anything that shines. In fading light, you might see the eyes of a spider hiding under a log, as the facets of their little night-vision eyes reflect more light than their surroundings.

447 **Take a natural feature** vacation. Travel to see a geological wonder instead of a man-made one. Yellowstone National Park has a Disney-like assortment of natural attractions, such as bubbling mud and geysers, all courtesy of geothermal energy. Travel to see an active volcano in Hawaii, the aftermath of the eruption at Mount St. Helens, or Craters of the Moon National Monument in Idaho, where you can walk on lava rock.

ADOPT A CLOUD

Be intimate with the clouds today. Look at them closely. Notice the infinite varieties. Tattered, firm, protruding, plump, flat, wispy, tall, dark...like potential lovers, they come in all shapes and sizes. Examine them all and find the ones that attract you most.

A few cloud basics will help you join clouds on their adventures. There are three basic categories of clouds: cirrus clouds are the highest wisps, stratus clouds are mid- and low-level sheets, and cumulus clouds are puffy clouds that start as fluffs of cotton and billow to towering heights. That's all the information you need to deepen your exploration of clouds and to discover a new living world that is yours to enjoy by simply looking up.

448 Explore the subtleties of overcast.
Don't just make a quick glance out your window and give up on the weather when the sky is gray. Go outside and look closely at the intricate textures

overhead. Is the overcast composed of pillows of white like a sheet of cotton? Or is the sky simply an immobile murky fog, suspended overhead? We love bright blue skies and vibrant orange sunsets, but much of the sky is made up of shades of gray. Pause to examine today's overcast and you'll see that every gray day is different and worthy of a closer look.

449 **Look through the overcast** to the sun on the other side. Trust that it will energize you, even though the overcast layer shields the two of you from connecting. Even in dark and dreary weather, imagine the crisp blue sky just above the cloud cap. Learn to judge the thickness of the overcast layers by the amount of light that penetrates. Sometimes, you'll see blue through cracks in thin overcast. Occasionally, a window will open in an overcast layer only to reveal another overcast layer above. Learn to discover the layered architecture of the clouds above you. Get a window seat on your next commercial flight and look inside the layers as you pass through them, so that you can better understand what you see from the ground.

450 **Spend a day at the beach,** even when you're trapped inland under an overcast sky. That cloud deck above is made of the same moisture you would see at the ocean. Notice how the overcast is moving just like the waves. Once you understand that clouds are ocean water in the sky, even if you're landlocked, you can enjoy a day at the beach simply by looking up.

451 **Let the sky be your conduit** to adventurous and distant places. That same sky above your building connects you with your dream location. Follow it to your fantasy spot. Imagine that you could walk on the carpet of overcast overhead to that island beach, and lower yourself down to enjoy the surf. Spend a minute there and come back to your day at work refreshed.

452 **Explore the height** of the clouds just as you would a mountain range. You'll find the tallest peaks in thunderstorms, where towering cumulus clouds often grow to more than twice the height of Mt. Everest. Look for these cloud mountains building on hot and humid summer days, especially when a cold front is forecast to pass through. Gaze to the tall clouds as you would at the Himalayas or the Tetons in the distance. Notice the varied hues that reflect off the contours of their snow-capped peaks. It's no accident that these clouds often grow the tallest in strong Midwestern storms. This way, even flatlanders can enjoy the majestic splendor of mountains all summer long, courtesy of the clouds.

453 **Tune in to the natural light** so that a change in brightness outside alerts you that clouds are on the move. Whenever your internal light meter registers a change, peer out your window with curiosity. Did a rogue cumulus cloud obliterate the

sun for just a moment? Or did a giant overcast layer steamroll the blue sky and cover the sun for the day? Develop your sensitivity to changes in the light and you'll be more in touch with the natural cycles of the weather and the movements of the clouds.

454 Watch the clouds dance. You've seen puffy cumulus clouds float across the sky, but you may not have noticed that almost all clouds move. Even a cloud that remains stationary over a mountain peak is actually alive, with equal amounts of new cloud forming and old cloud dissolving in a continuous dance. Entire sheets of overcast usually march across the sky. That which looked like a stagnant cap on your day is actually often propelled by strong, high-altitude winds. Spend an extra minute detecting the movement of clouds overhead. See if the clouds always come from the same direction.

455 **Watch clouds materialize** out of thin air. On a clear blue morning on your way to work, look for the first puffy cumulus cloud to appear. Keep checking, because once you see the first kernel of white, more clouds are likely to materialize. Be like a kid over a hot pot of oil full of little golden popcorn kernels. Watch the sky with fascination, as you wait to see if something delicious will emerge. Once the clouds pop, follow their journey. Are they getting bigger and rising? Are they blowing apart? Blackening? Keep an eye on your new companions from your office window and follow their voyage.

456 **Tune in** to the ups and downs of a day in the life of a cloud. Clouds depict a map of energy in the sky. As the sun heats the new day, air and energy is rising into new cumulus clouds. As the clouds blacken and showers begin, the energy that has risen into the clouds falls back to the earth in the form of rain or snow. Just like your ups and downs, the highs and lows are temporary. The daily energetic adventure of the clouds is a constant reminder that energy is always moving in your life, even when you feel completely stuck.

457 Chase a puffy cloud as it floats through your neighborhood, just as a child might when the first blimp or hot-air balloon glided through. Jump on your bike and race it through your neighbor's yard. Or open your sunroof and chase it across town. Follow its path and wish it farewell on its journey through your state. See if you can stay in the cloud's shadow for its entire trip through town.

458 Get your head into a cumulus cloud and try to envision its inner flow. We've all seen these puffy clouds growing and shrinking, but they are also rotating in a swirling motion. Can you tell if their inner flow is clockwise, counterclockwise, or a combination of both? Watch the edges and look for

circular motion as the perimeter boils over. Think of cumulus clouds rolling across the sky. Watch the subtle shapes and swirls and know that your life, too, is subtly swirling and changing in every moment. The clouds mirror your adventure.

459 **Be a cloud farmer** and watch your crops grow into unusual shapes and sizes. Take a lawn chair outside and watch the clouds parade past your personal viewing stand, as though you were the balloon judge for the Thanksgiving Day parade. No two clouds are the same. Fall in love with the giant mouse that floats through the sky against the brilliant blue backdrop. Notice a billowing, boiling marshmallow and follow it on its marshmallow flight. Find the beautiful reclining woman as she parades past. Notice that iceberg; could it be the same one that sank the *Titanic*? Clouds play a continuous movie for you to enjoy, even when you are stopped at a traffic light in the city. Look up and watch a preview of today's flick. Enjoy your own private

thirty-second screening, right through your sunroof, while you wait for the light to change.

460 Create your own soundtrack as the clouds float overhead. Hum to the drone of the overcast as it engulfs your town like a machine. Give each cloud its own theme music. Play Wagner or Beethoven as a storm builds, play Mozart when the clouds are puffy and the sky is blue, or try jazz when the day is soft.

461 Shift your focus away from the actual setting of the sun. Instead, discover the way the clouds are illuminated during the entire hour leading up to the sunset and the entire hour immediately afterward. Clouds are canvases for the subtle changes of light leading up to and immediately after the sunset.

462 Discover cirrus clouds. These high wisps of cloud in the upper atmosphere sometimes mean that bad weather is approaching within a day or two. They are often blown into ghostly wisps by extremely high winds. They make an entirely new textured landscape up high, which invites you to look up and beyond the challenges that seem to be right in your face. These beautiful threads of ice crystals are the last thing you would pass on your way out into space on the space shuttle and the first thing you would see when you looked back on Earth through the window. The cirrus clouds are your reminders that there is an adventure bigger than you out there, all the time, just overhead.

463 Study clouds at night. Watch them glide past the moon, backlit by the perfect wattage. Notice how the moon only illuminates them from above, while the sun primarily illuminates clouds after it reflects off the ground. As clouds of varying thickness pass in front of the moon, you'll discover a new array of colors and moonlit cloud canyons only visible at night.

BE YOUR OWN WEATHERMAN

Air is always on an adventure, courtesy of the weather. Temperature, pressure, and humidity are always changing. Weather systems are always moving faster or slower than forecast. Try as we might to predict the weather, it constantly defies prediction. Weather is one of the most adventurous forces in our everyday life because it is exclusively about change. Learn how it works and you'll become more at ease with change in your own life.

Every object in your life takes on a different identity as the weather changes. The road to work looks one way in a snowstorm and quite another just after the rain. Even the scenery in your front yard looks different in a thunderstorm than on a clear summer night. Weather changes the look of everything we know to be constant in our lives. Weather can train you to find a new adventure every day, simply by looking at the air that greets you each time you step outside.

Weather is made up of fair-weather (high-pressure systems) and rainy-weather (low-pressure systems). Cold and warm fronts, which are nothing more than boundaries between air masses, trail off the highs and lows. Get familiar with the normal flow of highs, lows, and fronts through your region. The more comfortable you are with their routine nature as they cross the country, the more you can accept highs and lows in your own life as a natural and recurring phenomenon.

464 Look for subtle changes in the temperature and barometric pressure. Get a small thermometer for the zipper pull of your jacket. Check the temperature regularly, just as you would check the time, to see if a front has passed through. Get a wristwatch with a barometer and watch the pressure rise and fall. As you learn to appreciate the subtle weather

changes throughout the day, you'll learn to better appreciate the subtle changes in your everyday life.

465 Get ready for a wild ride when the weatherman says that a cold front will be passing through your town. Winds may howl and the clouds will race across sky. As the midday sun heats the ground, the swirling clouds could firm up and darken as they come together. Then it might sprinkle or rain, before the clouds dissipate and a whole new cycle begins again. Throughout the day after a cold front passes, the air is extremely turbulent, and is mixing in a boiling flow. You can almost see the clouds bubble. Can you feel it on the ground? Everything is moving, not just blowing in the wind but moving up and down as well. Even from your office window you can enjoy the cycles of the day, as the cumulus clouds build and dissipate. Look for beautiful blue canyons in the sky, which will fill with white as the clouds grow together and open once again as they dissipate.

466 **The first day** after a cold front passes, the sky will often fill with puffy white cumulus clouds. On the second day, you'll usually see crystal-clear blue skies without a cloud in sight. And on the third day, winds will often shift toward the southwest, blowing in warm, moist air and reducing visibility. This is a crude description of sometimes-complex weather patterns, but see if you can follow the basic rhythm of a cold front as I've described it. Once you watch this weather pattern in motion, each day becomes its own season. You can celebrate the cloud cycles on day one and look forward to the clear blue on day two. On day three, you'll know to expect increasing humidity. As you master your secret understanding of the weather, a glance out the window to see what's new becomes a private adventure.

467 **Feel the heat shut off.** Year-round, the weather generally settles between 4 and 7 P.M. The sun is lower on the horizon and no longer heats the earth to the same degree. See if you can you feel the heat fading and the cool air settling all around you. As the evening closes in, air starts to sink into valleys and small depressions, like the one out by my mailbox. After a glorious day feeling the air rise into the boiling clouds, welcome the calming blanket of air that sinks as the heat shuts off. Watch the wind calm down, the clouds thin out, and the evening settle into a calm peace.

468 A thunderstorm is an adventurous event that comes right to your door. Turn off the lights, go to the window, lie down, and watch. Inside the core of the towering thunderstorm cloud is a tremendous amount of energy, rising and falling. Imagine that inside this one storm right outside your window is more energy than you will expend in your entire lifetime, exercising, running to complete errands, scrambling to check off items on your "to do" list. Sit and relax. Watch the adventure of the storm. Let it percolate and boil so you don't have to. Enjoy its busy adventure as it goes from birth to maturity...and then dissipates.

469 **Make your own rain gauge** by taking an empty container and scoring it with marks one-quarter inch apart on the inside. Put it outside and notice the uniqueness of every rainy day. Never again should rain be a one-word definition. Get to know the difference between the showers that often accompany a cold front and the steady rain that comes with a warm front. Just another rainy day gets really exciting when you know exactly how much rain the system has produced and what has to happen for the rain to stop. Every storm has slightly different features. Use your new rain gauge to explore the difference.

470 **Meet "Virga."** This is precipitation that evaporates before it reaches the ground. It looks like black smoke around and just beneath clouds when it is rain and white smoke when it is snow. Virga is another beautiful feature of the skyscape, and can often reflect light in a brilliant way to make a turbulent, cumulus-cloud day that much more exciting. When virga flows all the way to the ground, you are looking at rain or snow in the distance that may be coming your way. Try to judge its movement. Appreciate the fact that you can see something that others can't.

471 **We know that every snowflake** is unique. What about every raindrop? What is unique about each drop's shape, volume, and temperature? Go on a raindrop adventure; catch some with your tongue and see if in fact each drop is singular.

472 **Explore the fog.** The next time your neighborhood becomes a magic kingdom of dense moisture, cut your way through it, probing deeper and deeper into the unknown. Even though you've been down your street hundreds of times before, in the fog your block takes on an entirely new identity, muted and dampened. Notice how the fog digests sound and light. The thick moisture muffles even a car alarm. The streetlights

take on a muted glow. Go outside and bathe in the thick cream of the fog. Marvel as it erases your backyard like magic.

473 **Become a connoisseur** of blue. Name the subtle variations of what you previously called plain blue sky. Is it royal, midnight, pale, or robin's egg? Don't just be dismissive of the vast clear sky around you. Expand your color palette.

474 **Get outside frequently.** No matter what you do in your day, take five-minute breaks to go outside. Spend the first five minutes of every hour out in front of your office building. See if you can detect the subtle changes since your last visit. Record them. Follow them. Get to know the magic that is unfolding right outside your office building every day of the week.

475 Make your own forecast. Many

plans are ruined because the forecast called for rain, but the front passed through with no moisture, or the brief shower at noon was all the rain you are going to see. Don't waste energy getting angry with the weatherman. Instead, try to understand why he or she is wrong and you'll be free to make your own microforecast so you can enjoy your day without him. Get comfortable disagreeing with the forecast. Remember that the forecast is never as accurate as what you see out your window.

476 Discover the portion of the day when

the sky seems most magical. For me, it's the hour immediately after sunset, as the sky fades through the darkest shades of blue and finally becomes black. My whole body relaxes as the day relaxes into night. Determine your special hour of the day and adjust your schedule so you can be outside to enjoy it.

MOVE LIKE THE WIND

The wind has the power to transport us into the arms of nature. Even in a completely urban environment, the wind pierces our clothes as it blows down city blocks, embracing us with air from someplace else. In the dirtiest parts of New York City, the south breeze brings in moist marine air and with it comes the smell and feeling of the sea. When the northwest wind rips through New York, you can feel the presence of a farm in the Hudson Valley or perhaps an apple orchard in the Catskills. Examine the wind to see where it has been. It does not start five blocks up or downtown, only to blow the local dust in your eyes; it comes from perhaps hundreds of miles away and with it come the fibers of everything in its path.

As such, the wind is your ticket to adventure. When you can dissect it and sense its components, you have the ability to see and feel all things touched by the wind and to let those components envelop you. Even if you can't sense the literal pieces of the wind, trust that the exhaled breath of every human being is carried on the wind. Imagine that the last exhalation of every creature that has ever lived is also carried in the wind. And consider that the air that feeds all creatures to create new life is carried by the wind. Suddenly, you begin to realize that the wind is like the pulse of the entire Earth. And it is yours to forever enjoy, whether you hear it outside your window or feel it caress your skin.

477 Put a weather vane on your house.

A simple indicator on the cupola or flag pole on your property will at least allow you to observe the direction of the wind. An inexpensive weather station (available from many mail-order gadget companies) will allow you to make more detailed wind measurements. Make sure the anemometer has a peak gust indicator, so even if you never leave your home, you can still marvel at the strength of gusts that blow down your block. As a bonus, you'll learn to equate the sound of the gusts with their actual speed.

478 Become a weather vane. Practice

sensing the wind with your body. Feel the direction with the fine hairs on your skin. Notice which side of your face the wind is hitting. Toss up some weeds or cut grass to be sure; they will blow downwind. Train your senses to detect the wind without aid. Once you know the wind direction, you can much better forecast the weather, based on changes in your local airflow.

479 Learn to read a new language.

Look for the effects of the wind, even if you can't feel or hear it while you're inside your car or office. The leaves on tree branches will shimmer when the wind makes them twitch. About fifteen miles per hour of wind will make a flag fly out straight, like a solid sheet. Every smokestack is a wind indicator that will tell you the wind strength and direction at different altitudes. Notice the path of the smoke as it departs the stack. A straight vertical column indicates no wind. A trail of smoke that starts out vertically and gradually bends more downwind means that the wind gets stronger the higher you go.

480 **Watch leaves fall.** Look at them swirl and flip. What do they say about the air currents in your yard? Are they steady? Gusty? Is the air moving differently at different heights right on your property?

481 **Any body of water teaches** you volumes about the wind. Gauge the height of the ripples on the water—they will tell you the strength of the breeze. Dark patches indicate the strongest winds. Whitecaps form on the tops of waves when the wind blows in excess of about sixteen miles per hour. See if you can tell the direction of the wind as you look at the orientation of the waves. Look for cat's-paws on any body of water. These are patches of ripples that indicate gusts touching down on the surface of the water. They

allow you to track the varying speed and direction of the wind as it moves across a pond, lake, or swimming pool.

482 **Pause to listen** to the wind whenever it's windy, with all your attention focused on its sound. Listen for the various notes of the wind's symphony. Hear the intensity rise and fall, like ocean waves.

483 **Be the wind** throughout your day. Permeate your life as though you are a constant breeze. Find your way into all the places where you've found resistance. Breeze through your life with the effortless grace of the wind. Harness the wind's quiet power to move through or around almost anything in its path.

484 **Imagine** that the wind picks up the energy of everything it touches. A westerly breeze has blown through the entire country before it reaches an

East-Coast home. What if it picks up the energy of every crop, person, and animal by the time it reaches your door? Breathe in some of that energy as the wind permeates your clothes. Use the wind as fuel as you journey through your day. And exhale with power, knowing that you are sending the wind on another lap around the globe.

485 **Notice wind** that seems to come from out of nowhere. When you feel a strong gust, and a thunderstorm is nearby, it is probably air descending from the towering clouds and overpowering the prevailing winds. When you feel a similar rogue gust, and thunderstorms are not visible, you're probably feeling a thermal, which is a mini tornado of warm rising air. Look for leaves and dust rising in a circular flow. In the Southwest, strong thermals pull up so much dust that they are called dust devils. In the East, look for birds circling, taking a free ride on that rising air.

486

What does the wind bring? Why is it blowing? Is it warmer air, colder air, or more of what you already have? Wind is the mixer of all the air on the planet. Wind is the equalizer of two neighboring weather systems that have different atmospheric pressures. The wind is constantly working to create equality among air masses. Where can you create equality today?

487

The wind is pure adventure because it always has an unknown outcome. It peaks in gusts a little higher, flipping up a new leaf, or blowing down a weakened tree. Who knows what the next gust will bring? Let the wind remind you of the unknown outcome of your life. Live your adventurous day with the spirit of the wind; be an instrument of change, unpredictable, always about to gust a bit stronger and ready forever to go someplace new.

488 Learn to sail.

The type of boat is not important, but find a way to feel the wind actually propel you. Listen to the hull of the boat gurgle as you accelerate, powered by nature with seemingly no effort. Take a windsurfing lesson. Or head to your local yacht club and put up a sign that says "Crew Available." You might get to enjoy a weekend of racing or perhaps even an ocean sailing trip.

489 Get up into the wind.

Most flight schools offer inexpensive demo flights in small planes. You'll even have an opportunity to operate the controls and to feel the wind in three dimensions. Go for a glider ride. Or post a sign at any small airport that you would be willing to help wash airplanes in exchange for rides. Get to know your neighborhood from the air. All your local natural features will seem much more special.

BE A TREE

It's easy to take trees for granted and to lump them into one generic category. Trees, like humans, all look fundamentally the same. But as you look closer, you discover that there are infinite varieties and subtle distinctions that will forever surprise you.

I have always been in love with beautiful wooden furniture, boxes, and bowls. But only when I moved to a house adjacent to a forest and started making my own wooden bowls did I fall in love with trees. I had caressed many a burled wooden jewelry box or bird's-eye maple tabletop. But I never imagined that I could find such wood in my own backyard. When I started to understand what the woods I most cherished looked like in natural form, suddenly the trees became magical gifts. And now every time I am lucky enough to discover a burl-covered tree that has fallen in high winds, I harvest a bountiful treasure for free.

The world of trees provides a readily accessible adventure. And since it seems so innocuous on the surface, exploration of a forest is actually that much more intriguing. As you gain knowledge of the trees, you'll discover their world. You can see it on the side of the highway as you drive to work, on a walk in a nature preserve, or even on a walk through your backyard.

490 **Find your tree-mate.** Perhaps she is on your property or somewhere on the entrance ramp of the highway that leads to your office. Pull over and put on your flashers. Notice what she is doing today. Notice her leaves emerging in the spring or fading to a lighter green later in the summer. Notice where she bends when the wind blows. Look at her in the sunlight and moonlight. Make this tree your own and stop for just thirty seconds every day to notice what's new with your tree.

491 **Give your tree** her own calendar and mark major events. Watch her move through the seasons. Every year, she will surprise you. Buds will come out early one year. Or leaves will fall late. Compare notes every year, as you watch your new friend's magic constantly unfolding.

492 **Bring peak fall foliage** fascination to spring season. Notice which trees bud first. In the Northeast, a red spring mist emerges on every hillside as maple trees bloom. It takes about two weeks for the flowers to emerge, peak, and then fall to the ground, in a cycle every bit as beautiful as the emergence of peak fall colors. Each species of tree puts on a slightly different show. Don't wait for the leaves to be fully revealed before you notice spring in the trees. Watch varied buds emerging throughout the early spring and celebrate their arrival.

493 **Look closely,** after the flowers have fallen, for the leaves to push forward and unroll like magic. Each day, they come more into view, in a brilliant display of natural creation. Notice the phases of this emergence and the vibrant, virgin green of the new leaves, as they first unfurl.

494 **Find the leaf** that fits you like a glove. It's easy to imagine that leaves are the hands of trees when you look at the veins of any leaf and notice how they mirror the pattern of veins on the back of your own hand. Look for fingers that match your own. Silver maple leaves have long and skinny fingers, while red maples have stubbier fingers in a tighter pattern. If your hand were a leaf, what kind would it be? Imagine that all leaves are waving to you as you walk or drive past a tree. Wave back!

495 **Discover bark.** It's slightly different on each species of tree. On ash trees you'll find the bark in a diamond pattern; on beeches, the bark is smooth; and on shagbark hickories, the bark is, of course, shaggy. As you begin to learn how to identify

trees by their bark, you'll notice that the bark is slightly different on every single tree, even in a grove full of the same species. Every tree has it's own "face," and like humans, each face is just a bit different. As you come to appreciate the beauty of every tree, you'll also start to see every person as a beautiful work of nature, regardless of the configuration of his or her face or body.

496 **Every tree is an opportunity** for a treasure hunt. Look for burls, unusual tumor-like bulges on the trunks and branches. Look for holes, in which animals may live, and notice the bark patterns around the edges of these holes. Sometimes they look like hearts or lips. Scan the limbs for squirrel nests, which are piles of leaves perched up high. Look for wood shavings, the telltale sign of woodpeckers poking away, searching for bugs beneath the bark. Look for vines climbing the trees (watch out for poison ivy). Get to know every inch of a tree, and always be ready to discover something new.

497

Get in the habit of scanning trees for guests. Along the shoreline, look for the striking silhouettes of egrets or herons. In the plains, look for birds of prey. And look for owls perched in New England forests just after the sun goes down. Allow more time to get to your destination so you can scan branches that line the road. Perhaps you'll spot a turkey vulture perched overhead. And when it takes off, finds a thermal, and soars one hundred feet above your head in under a minute with barely a flap, in that moment, you'll be to flying too.

498

Use your hands as well as your eyes to explore the joints where branches fuse into the trunk of a tree. Every branch connects differently, at a different angle, with a different supporting structure above and below the joint. Compare the trees' angles and joints with those of a person. Admire the way branches join the body of a tree the same way you might admire the glorious shoulders of your lover.

499 **Step back and look** at the outline of a tree as you would a sculpture. How is the canopy shaped? How long is the trunk? Each tree has a powerful profile and unique outline, worthy of an art museum. But this museum is free, always open, and no travel is needed to visit. Every tree is a new canvas to examine and appreciate.

500 **Look at the trees** immediately after the rain. Some bark absorbs moisture and darkens while other bark repels water and shimmers. Rain gives an otherwise plain gray tree a brilliant variety of new colors and textures. Notice the way that lichens on the bark brighten with fresh moisture. Look for droplets hanging off the limbs and for buds that have captured an entire drop. A tree that would previously go unnoticed takes on a new identity after the rain.

501 **Study tree roots.** Look at their texture, wrinkles, and bulges. Follow them from the trunk of the tree as they reach out to connect with the earth. Notice how the roots conform to their surroundings. Notice how they generally configure to stabilize and support the mass of their particular tree. If you could grow roots today when you arrived at your office or home, how would they look?

502 **Watch trees reach for the sky.** Follow their branches upward and notice how they thin out near the top. Trees show us a powerful balance between grounding in the earth and reaching outward, beyond our known boundaries. Trees are simultaneously heavy in their roots and light in their wispy branches. They demonstrate the balance that matters most in life. Grow a few more roots if you are feeling scattered. Reach further outside your boundaries if you are feeling shut down. Let trees teach you a new way to both ground and soar in your everyday life.

503 **Dance with a tree** in the wind. Look at how it bends with grace in a smooth arc, more at the top and less near its roots. No matter how strong the wind, the tree is usually able to withstand the force, even if it loses some of its smaller branches. Let a tree teach you how to withstand forces beyond your control. Flex like a tree. Bend like a tree. Be pliable, resilient, and compliant like a tree. Mesh effortlessly with your neighbors as though you were in a tight grove of trees in the wind.

504 **Bond with a tree.** Rub your hand on the bark. Hug it. Lie down on a big root and see if you can feel energy flowing up from the ground to feed its limbs. Climb one. Build a tree house in your backyard.

505 **Let a tree touch you.** Touching a tree is very different from having a tree touch you. On a windy day, sit on a rock next to a tree with a limb gently touching your body. As the wind moves the tree, the branch will rub against you, like a loving cat rubbing up against your leg.

506 **Let a tree teach you** how to embrace your scars. When a tree loses a limb, scar tissue heals over the wound to make an unusual piece of natural artwork. Every trunk is covered with such scars, each a unique hieroglyph. Notice these beautiful marks on the trunks of trees and practice similar appreciation of the unique scars on your body.

507 **Spend half an hour** just sitting among the trees. Don't eat, read, talk on your cell phone, or do anything other than just sit. Find a comfortable place in the woods, away from other people and activity. Set a timer and just stay put. At first, your mind may swirl with all the things you would rather be doing or need to do when you get home or back to the office. Keep noticing what life is like for a tree. Notice everything the tree notices; loose bark flapping on an adjacent tree, branches meshing with a neighbor in the gusts of wind, buds emerging, birds landing on branches. Spend thirty minutes in a tree's world, just to see what it would feel like to trade places.

508 **Search for the silver** in smooth tree branches. Look closely as you stare through the trees. Observe that light reflects off certain limbs with a silver tone. Once you detect this magical quality, all forests start to shimmer with the reflective brilliance of silver, even on a cloudy day.

509 **Discover the leaf soup** that lines every path through the woods, after all the leaves have fallen from the trees. The leaves of many species are equalized in a natural jumble. Notice the lack of discrimination. All colors, all shapes, and all sizes

have come together with equal weight on the ground floor, where they will decay together as one.

510 **Find gold** buried on the forest floor after the winter snow melts. Soften your focus and look at the carpet of leaves with a squint. The brown and tan patina of old leaves will take on a golden color. Once you see this wealth of organic matter with new eyes, the forest will be forever covered with gold.

511 **Meet the beeches.** These trees, when saplings, keep their leaves through the winter. In March or April, they shed their shriveled tan leaves, as new green sprouts appear and leaves unroll for another year. Young beech trees extend the season of leaf watching through the winter.

512 **All the fallen leaves** on your property are yours to enjoy. Notice the infinite sizes and shapes—like snowflakes, but they don't melt. If leaves were legal tender, you would be very rich indeed. Spend them freely, as you bag them and put them by the curb. Rake through your fortune, like a prince or princess. Who cares if a few large bills are taken by the wind? And when the city comes to suck up the pile in front of your house, or when you take all fifteen bags of leaves to the dump, you get to practice letting go of the wealth you accumulated over the past year. But the leaves are infinitely abundant and will once again fill your yard. What if money is equally abundant? Perhaps the leaves can teach you to experience the flow of money in and out of your life with the same sense of freedom.

513 **Stop and listen** to the sounds of the woods. On your way home from work, find a quiet road, pull over, and lie down on a blanket on the hood of your car, leaning on the windshield. Close your eyes and just listen. Savor the sounds of nature, right on the side of the road, alive with unpredictable energy and adventure. Even if you just pull over, recline your seat and open your windows and sunroof; you'll still enjoy the magic whisper of the natural world.

FLOW LIKE A RIVER

Visit a river of any size. You don't need to go to the Colorado or Amazon. Even a small stream through your neighborhood will do just fine. Moving water is a powerful teacher that will enhance your life. Find a local source and get acquainted.

Return with regularity and watch the river flow through time. Ideally, your river will have a swimming hole, which you can dive into year after year. As you sit on a rock and feel the power of the water flowing past you, you can assess the changes you've experienced since last year's swim. All the significant circumstances of the past year seem quite insignificant in comparison to the timeless flow of the water, which lived long before you were born and will flow long after you are dead.

Rivers teach us how to be adventurous by demonstrating the art of surrender. The water is in a constant state of letting go. There is no attachment as the water makes its journey downstream. There are eddies and stagnant pools on the way; perhaps these are the river's healthy outlet for fear and indecision. But by and large, the river flows onward without editorial comment. With no apparent knowledge of the outcome, it flows downstream with abandon, and provides a powerful model for an adventurous daily life.

514 Eat lunch with a river. Make it a regular monthly meeting, you and your river, and note your friend's small changes on every meeting. Get to know its levels. Watch it rise and fall, like your life. As the quantity of water in a river changes, watch the river effortlessly adapt. When the water is low, small rivulets dry up and only the main flow is intact. When the

volume of water swells after the rain, side streams fill once again. Notice how the river seems unconditionally at ease, regardless of its volume. Make sure you continue to visit in the winter, so you can watch the river freeze into unusual sculptures. Season after season, it flows on.

515 **Sit by a stream** and see how many features you notice. Scan the surrounding rocks, eroded and polished by the incessant flow of water. Watch tiny drops of spray curl off the top of each waterfall, misting the adjacent lichen. Notice how falling water gets aerated and how bubbles are constantly moving downstream. Try to feel the air moved out of the way by the moving water. Every river puts on an elaborate show for you to enjoy, if you take the time to sit and watch.

516 **Listen to a river.** Sit alongside, or on a rock in the middle, with the river as your companion. Notice the sounds of all the different flows, from the tiniest ripples to actual drop-offs. Close your eyes and listen to the moving water in stereo. See if you can decipher water moving at a different pace in each ear. Sit so that two distinct rhythms converge in the center of your head, as though you were listening on perfectly adjusted headphones. Let this be your personal sound-track of calmness.

517 **Let a river be your mentor;** it will listen to you with unconditional support. Tell it your problems and challenges, and sing songs to it. Imagine that the river is there to hear you whenever you are feeling most alone. Allow the river to carry your problems downstream and to digest them in its ongoing flow.

518 **Cross a stream** in your bare feet, either hopping from rock to rock, or boldly walking on the riverbed. Learn impermanence from the river. You can never step into the same river twice—even on the return trip, you'll be crossing a different river. The river mirrors all of life and reminds us that everything is constantly moving. Our problems are part of the flow and so are our accomplishments. Even our feelings constantly flow through us; pain moves through to make way for pleasure, which makes way for more pain once again. We don't possess our sadness, fear, or joy, even though we sometimes feel like we are consumed by these emotions. Feelings flow like a river. Everything in life eventually flows onward.

519 Follow a river downstream, and observe the tenacious path of river water. Notice how it bumps into obstacles and wastes no time flowing in a new direction, only to join with the larger flow and continue its journey downstream. Look for branches and forks in the flow and admire the easy determination of the water. Take that energy with you in your everyday life.

520 **Discover the different textures** of a river. Look for glassy sections, even though the surrounding water is rough. Look for intricate patterns of ripples, each one different. See if you can read the texture of the bottom of the river as you observe the texture of the ripples on the surface.

521 **Look for the smallest** waterfall. A drop of just one inch will sometimes show you a perfect sheet of smooth laminar flow. Treat the one- and two-foot drops in your local stream like your own personal waterfalls, full of rich sounds if you'll stop to listen. You can slither right up to your mini-falls on your back and watch the cascade, just inches from your face. And you won't have to fight with other tourists, clamoring for a picture or a parking space. We are often only interested in the biggest and the best. Search for the smallest and see if a new world opens up. Once you get comfortable with both extremes, every waterfall has something to offer, regardless of the size.

522 Discover eddies, pools of river water stuck in a circular flow. Throw a small stick in an eddy and watch it make laps. Are you in an eddy in your life? Or part of the larger flow?

523 Walk the length of a river, from start to finish. Better still, float downstream in a kayak, inner tube, or canoe. You'll see an entirely new side of your town once you float through it.

RIDE THE OCEAN WAVES

Everyone becomes an explorer at the beach. We can stand up against the edge of another world full of creatures and forces unlike anything we experience on land. The ocean is the most open expanse on the planet. Yet we have none of the natural equipment needed to live in the ocean; we can't breathe, hear, see, or propel ourselves in the sea without assistance. We are left to speculate what life is like for the creatures that make the ocean their home.

The Earth is made up of a much greater percentage of ocean than land mass. But we don't know the ocean nearly as well as we know the ground on which we live. And so the edge of the ocean is a very special place. It is the transitional zone between hard land and the soft water. It is the closest most people can come to seeing what lies just beyond the horizon. And it is a place to play with the forces present when land meets water. All this is available to the beautiful accompaniment of the waves.

524 **Try to feel the edge** of the country approaching before you actually arrive at the ocean. The coast feels different from the interior. How soon can you sense it? Do you need to see the ocean in order to feel it? Or does your intuitive sense tell you that you are near? Don't focus so much on your destination during your long drive to the shore. Instead, see if you can focus on the subtle clues that the shore is fast approaching.

525 **Have a friend blindfold you** on a drive to the beach and walk you right up to the water's edge. Remove the blindfold so that your first sight is the ocean waves. Burn that image into your mind, so you can readily recreate the peaceful wonder of the ocean anytime you like.

526 **Go into the water** and feel the power of the ocean. Dive through the waves as they roll over your head. Learn to bodysurf. Or just stand in the water up to your knees and feel the ocean pull you in and out. Our bodies are primarily composed of water. In the ocean, see if you feel as if you are finally home.

527 **Walk on the beach** in the off-season, when the crowds are thin and the light is beautiful. In the summer, the beach is ablaze with light and it's often too bright to see the beach's subtle beauty. But in the winter months, the sun makes a lower arc through the sky, which illuminates each grain of sand from its side and creates a new atmosphere.

528 **Go to the ocean** at least once each year for more than just a tan. Share the truth, either with yourself in a journal or out loud with someone you love. The sea and sand are pure and there's nothing that the waves can't digest. The ocean will support you to write or speak passionately.

529 **Explore the varied colors** of the ocean water. Look for new shades of gray, blue, green, and white. How do these colors compare to the colors of bark in the forest or the rock outcrop you pass on your way to work? Look for the same silver in the ocean that you see in the beech trees. Scan the distant ocean for the same colors you'd find in the sky. See if you can begin to discover the similarity between all the various canvases of nature's beauty.

530 **Pick up a handful of sand** and look at it closely. The power of the ocean waves has crumbled the shoreline into these fine grains. Notice the different colors. Can you imagine what the rocks and shells might have looked like before they were eroded into these very grains? Have someone bury you up to your neck in the sand just to feel the granules touch every inch of your body.

531 **Sit on the beach** facing into the wind and notice the unique quality of the sea air. How does it feel compared to the wind that blows through the forest? Is it wet? Does it taste salty? See if you can feel the long ocean journey made by the wind. Perhaps it traveled thousands of miles, creating and caressing waves on its way to your face.

532 **Get to know the ocean's** varied moods. Visit the beach at sunrise and watch how it awakens. Stroll on the beach in steady rain and watch it flatten out the waves. Head to the beach in a storm to see the fierce power of the sea. Go to the beach when it snows, just to see what happens to the flakes when they hit the water. Most people only go to the beach for the midday sun, but the ocean has infinite moods to discover.

533 Try a night of moon bathing.

Check your local paper for the time of the moonrise. Bring your beach blanket and all your normal accessories. Take binoculars and scan the surface of the moon for the biggest craters. See if you can feel the moon's pull on the tides within your body. Look for an iridescent halo around the moon. Parking is free and no sunscreen is needed. Instead of another night in front of the television or on the Web, go outside and marvel at the moon's beautiful journey across the sky, mirrored in the ocean and the sand.

534 **Lose your thoughts** in the sound of the surf. Give yourself twenty minutes to sit on the beach with your eyes closed to simply listen. Match your breath to the ocean's waves; inhale as the waves recede, exhale as the waves crash forward. Feel the sea exhale with you as each wave breaks on the shore. Let your thoughts and problems be dashed in the waves. The sea can teach you how to meditate.

535 **Look for new life forms.** On every visit to the beach, search for a previously unfamiliar creature. Not all seagulls are the same. Look closely in tidal pools for new life emerging. Search for baby crabs and freshly hatched bugs. Look for jellyfish that have washed ashore.

536 **Take something home** from the beach so you can recreate the spirit of the ocean in your home. Line your front path with driftwood, shells, or any other ocean artifact. Make your own art out of sea glass or anything else you find on your visit. Find a way to bring the ocean home. Don't kill or damage anything in the process; there is plenty of dead material that would otherwise be crumbled into sand.

537 Pick up a pocketful of trash from the shoreline on every visit. Look for plastic that the sea can't digest. Use this simple act as a small token of your respect for the ocean and a way to continue to deepen your relationship with nature. Even better, carry plastic grocery bags with you and clean up a bagful.

538 Look out across the largest body of water in your vicinity. It may be a pond, or an ocean with the nearest large landmass thousands of miles away. Look all the way across and consider how much water there is between you and someone like you standing on the other shore, looking your way. Send a message into the horizon. Put a message in a bottle and set it adrift, with an invitation for the recipient to call you.

539 **Look underwater.** Learn to snorkel or scuba dive. Ride in a glass-bottom boat. Do whatever is necessary to take a look at the vast array of creatures that live beneath the surface, even if you only visit the aquarium.

540 **Get a CD** of nothing but the sound of ocean waves. It will transport you to the ocean from your living-room floor, even though you are lying on your back thousands of miles from the coast. The disc will help you get lost in the ocean waves anytime you close your eyes.

541 **Paint your life story** in the sand. Use your feet like a paintbrush and make giant hieroglyphics in the sand to illustrate where you've been and where you hope to go. Make your pictographs so big that anyone flying overhead stops to circle and read them. Then ask the lifeguard if you can climb up high on his chair, so you can marvel at your impermanent work from a new perspective, as the wind and sea dissolve it.

AN ADVENTURE IN THE RAIN

It was raining so hard I had to put on my swim goggles just to walk to the pool. I stood alone and watched long drops fly through the air, pelting my body. It hurt.

I got in the water and submerged my head halfway up my goggles. There, I surveyed craters caused by tiny meteorites of water, which, upon impact, rolled into the larger body of the liquid Olympic pool. I lay on my back on the bottom, just four feet from the surface. I observed the drops from below, imagining what it feels like to be a fish going to work on a rainy day.

I swam the backstroke and sidestroke, and compared the different perspectives of the raindrop/swim-goggle collision. Like snowflakes, no two drops were the same. I tried to crawl between the ripples of the drops that had fallen in front of me. I stood with my tongue skyward, wondering if equatorial rainwater tastes different. It doesn't.

And the sound of the rain was a symphony.

It took me thirty hours to reach this particular swimming pool...in Guam. A good friend and airline employee had sent me a free ticket to join him for two weeks of some of the finest scuba diving in the world. We visited Truk lagoon, and dove through cargo holds full of torpedo parts aboard

WWII Japanese freighters, sunken in American air raids. In Palau, we tethered ourselves to an underwater ledge in a current strong enough to tear off our masks if we weren't careful. We watched hundreds of sharks chase marine life carried up from the deep ocean floor by this current. But the South Pacific adventure I remember most is swimming in my friend's swimming pool outside his apartment building...in the rain.

Only the simplest swim trunks and goggles were required for my simple adventure, in spite of the fact that I had lugged a heavy bag of scuba equipment with me on three different airplanes. Had I not worked so hard to travel so far from home, I might have missed it. I traveled ten thousand miles to find the simplicity of the rain.

conclusion:
a new
world of
adventure

My friend Tom tells a story about little brown birds. As he was growing up, he remembers seeing numerous little brown birds in his yard. Sparrows, he discovered, and from then on all little brown birds were sparrows. Over the next twenty years, the brown color became less significant in his mind and all little birds were simply sparrows. He had shut off all capacity in his brain to see any small bird as anything other than the little brown birds in his yard.

And then one day he was camping and noticed that one of the little brown birds actually had an orange belly. And another little brown bird had a red body and black wings. What was going on here? he thought. Have I just discovered a secret world here in these woods, flapping around my tent? When did all little birds stop being brown? He later found out that he had seen a Baltimore oriole and a scarlet tanager. In a flash, an entire world had opened up for him to discover, and now Tom can tell me the name of every songbird in the trees outside his house. He's passionate about the world of birds and now knows all their subtle differences.

Where are you locked in a world of little brown birds? Somewhere in your life there is a world of adventure for you to explore. All you need is an open mind.

This world that you have been missing applies all over your life. You might find your own little brown birds in the way that you breathe, in your relationship to spending money, in your relationship with some aspect of your life that you were sure you had figured out. But that piece of your world might just be a rich place for discovery. That dull marriage and that dull group of friends might actually be full of adventurous opportunity with the slightest shift of perspective.

I wish you a life rich in adventure, regardless of your circumstances or finances. I believe there is an innate childlike adventurer inside you. I have tried to give you ways to wake him or her up from the comfort, safety, and convenience of your own life. I hope that you will make your life more exciting and fun as a result of reading and using these adventures, and inventing more of your own. And that you'll never sell your inner adventurer short again.

ACKNOWLEDGMENTS

I could fill a whole book with the names of all the people who supported me to make this book a reality. Thank you to my many friends, teachers, and co-adventurers, too numerous to list. But a few in particular who stand out for sharing their generous wisdom and support are: David Dowd, Joe Cloidt, Adrienn Sztankovics, Tessa Gilmore Barnes, Mary Sinclair, Kim McKeever, Terry Sheriffs, Dayashakti, Judy Fox, Michael Levin, Claudia Cross, Deb Werksman, Peter Lynch, Katherine Braunschweig, Tom Wolff, Brian Harley, Josh Karlin, and Erika Tsoukanelis.

A special thanks goes out the Kieffabers; this entire book was written in their basement.

And thank you to every client who has included me as coach on their glorious life adventure. It has been an honor to be a trusted partner on your journey. Our work together helped make this book possible.

Finally, thanks to my parents, who, each in their own way, taught me to be adventurous.

ABOUT THE AUTHOR

David Silberkleit is a Master Certified Life Coach who has helped hundreds of people bring the spirit of adventure to everyday life. It was only after years of traditional adventures that he discovered the degree to which adventure is possible for everyone and anyone, regardless of their circumstances.

David holds six different pilot's licenses, is a certified scuba diver and ski instructor, is an avid rock climber, and has ridden his bike through thirteen different countries. His top ten traditional adventures include:

10. Scuba diving with sharks in Palau
 9. Biking from Hanoi to Saigon on a recumbent bike
 8. Breaking a concrete block with his fist in a karate test
 7. Climbing a rising air current in a sailplane to an altitude of 27,000 feet over Nevada

6. Flying instrument approaches in single-engine airplanes in bad weather with a low cloud ceiling and low visibility

5. Flying a blimp

4. Throwing out the first pitch at a Major League Baseball game in front of 52,000 people

3. Dining at the White House

2. Getting married to a long-time girlfriend on a farm in New Zealand and celebrating with the entire village in a softball game on the crop-duster landing strip (a motorcycle trip around Canada's Prince Edward Island later led to their divorce)

1. Strolling down Broadway in a Jughead costume in the Macy's Thanksgiving Day Parade

While searching for the ultimate route on a round-the-world tandem bike trip with his new girlfriend, David realized that wherever he went adventure was present. It suddenly became crystal clear to him that adventure is not something one finds externally but instead lives inside us all. He cut the bike trip short and came home to write books and to coach people to find vitality and courage in their lives right now, without waiting for weekends, vacation, or retirement.

David coaches local clients in person at his Connecticut office. He also supports clients around the world via telephone and email.

Visit www.everydayadventure.com for information about personal coaching, speaking engagements, and adventure seminars. At this site, you can also post your own everyday adventures, purchase an adventurous-life audio program, and sign up for a free daily adventure email.